*Words of praise from women who have
used and loved Dawn's book:*

"Prior to working with Dawn, my life in this area was
filled with sadness and despair. I was truly hopeless and
thought things would never change. Well, things did
change—I changed. I am no longer shackled by my choices
of yesterday. Today I have a sense of freedom I had never
known was possible. My spirit has been restored and my
life divinely altered. Now that is a powerful feeling!"

—LeLania McDaniel

"Dawn's program as outlined in this book has helped me
beyond measure, and I am forever grateful to her. Dawn
not only 'talks the talk,' but has 'walked the walk.'
Her story resonates with the reader."

—Joi Natiello

"Dawn's program was simple to follow while getting to the
source of my difficulties, teaching me how to deal with
them and then going on to create a happy, confident new
me. I am grateful to Dawn every day for giving me the
tools I need to find the life and the relationships I want."

—R.J. Carlson

FROM HEARTBREAK TO

Heart's Desire

DEVELOPING A HEALTHY GPS
(GUY PICKING SYSTEM)

♥

Dawn Maslar, MS

CENTRAL RECOVERY PRESS

CENTRAL RECOVERY PRESS
Central Recovery Press (CRP) is committed to publishing exceptional materials addressing addiction treatment, recovery, and behavioral health care, including original and quality books, audio/visual communications, and Web-based new media. Through a diverse selection of titles, it seeks to impact the behavioral health care field with a broad range of unique resources for professionals, recovering individuals and their families, and the general public. For more information, visit www.centralrecoverypress.com.

Central Recovery Press, Las Vegas, NV 89129
© 2010 by Dawn Maslar
All rights reserved. Published 2010.
Printed in the United States of America.

Publisher: Central Recovery Press
             3371 N. Buffalo Drive
             Las Vegas, NV 89129

16 15 14 13 12 11 10   1 2 3 4 5

ISBN-10: 0-9818482-6-5
ISBN-13: 978-0-9818482-6-6

Cover design and interior by Sara Streifel, Think Creative Design

Acknowledgments

I want to thank my dad. Besides being my one and only stockholder, he loved and encouraged me every step of the way.

Second, I want to thank my best friend, Ed. His love and support allowed me to pursue my dream (or, as he called it at times, my obsession).

Thank you, Vivian, for your loving guidance.

Thank you, Mom, for your love and support

Thank you, Karen Hillman at KarenHillman.com, for the beautifully done author photo.

Thank you, Granny, for your love and support.

I want to thank the wonderful women who gave their time to read, edit, and make suggestions: Michelle, Michele, Paula, and Jana. A special thanks to Mary, who spent her weekend doing my final edits.

Thank you, Hal Zina Bennett, my kind, diligent, and tactful editor.

Special thanks to Donna, who helped show me the path.

Thanks to Norbert, Jay, and the rest of the Davies writers' group.

Thank you, Helen O'Reilly, for your skillful editing.

Thank you, God, for giving me this opportunity and blessing.

Table of Contents

Introduction v

1   What's a Broken Picker, and What Does It Have to Do with My Broken Heart? 1

2   How Do You Break a Picker? 15

3   Healing Your Picker, Step by Step 23

4   Step One Personal Retreat 27

5   Step Two Taking Care of Yourself 41

6   Step Three Meditation: Getting Grounded 53

7   Step Four Journaling: Gaining Self-Knowledge 65

8   Step Five Positive Affirmations 75

9   Step Six Pamper Yourself: Loving Yourself 91

10   Step Seven Do Something New: Changing Your Beliefs 103

11   Step Eight Doing Something Good for Someone Else: Joy 115

12   Step Nine Review of You 125

13   Step Ten Dreamweaving 141

14   Step Eleven Plan-a-Man: Build Your Beau 149

15   Step Twelve Making a Vision Board 161

16   The Dating Guide 167

Resources 181

Introduction

Are you one of us women who gets her heart broken over and over again, unlike some others who seem to know how to attain their hearts' desires? Have you ever been told that you've got "a broken picker"? If so, take heart—your broken picker is what keeps you choosing the partners most likely to break your heart; but healing your broken picker is what this book is all about.

What's a picker?

Well, to begin with, it's that part of us that chooses the men in our lives, and when it's broken, that's trouble! Having a broken picker can be a very painful thing. Take it from me. I know. I once had a man jump onto the hood of my car, clutching the torn-out distributor wires and screaming, "Hah, you can't go anywhere now!" A person with a well-running picker might have leapt from the car, called the cops, or generally gotten away, fast. But no, not me. My broken picker took his actions as a sign that he must really love me—and I married him! That was husband number one, and the beginning of a string of disappointing relationships that were a sure sign that my picker was broken.

So how can you tell if you have a broken picker? Well, you might have a broken picker if:

- Your date wants to go back to your place…because he still lives with his mother.

- The man you just slept with didn't call you the next day…just like his five predecessors.

- You meet a man whose back is covered in tattoos of the names of all his ex-girlfriends…and you find yourself trying to figure out where he could put yours.

- The man you recently started dating calls to say he can't make the date, because his car just got repossessed.

- And you definitely have a broken picker if you tell him, "That's OK, I can drive."

You might also have a broken picker if:

- You are reading this thinking you *might* have a broken picker.

- You are reading this thinking, "It's not my picker. I just haven't found the right guy." (By the way, this is called denial.)

- You read these and laughed.

You also might have a broken picker if:

- You read these and didn't laugh.

CHAPTER ONE

What's a Broken Picker, and What Does It Have to Do with My Broken Heart?

"'TIS STRANGE WHAT A MAN MAY DO,
AND A WOMAN YET THINK HIM AN ANGEL."
—WILLIAM MAKEPEACE THACKERAY

*Y*our picker is not so much a thing as it is a feeling. It's that tingling feeling you get when you meet someone you like. You know what I mean; you walk into a room and you start scanning the area. All of a sudden, your focus is on him. You think, "Wow, he's cute!" A warm sensation moves up your body. Your heart starts beating faster and you feel flushed. You look around to see if anyone notices, and then you refocus. Your gaze travels over his physique, examining his face, his clothing, and his mannerisms. You find something unique that you really like—maybe he's wearing your favorite style of suit, or he has the big, strong hands that you just love. You even imagine how it would feel to be touched by them.

Although this is all occurring in just a brief moment, it is enough time for him to feel your presence. He turns and looks at you. Your breathing stops, and you feel your heart start racing as the blood rushes to your face. You feel faint. But then he smiles. You're excited and nervous as you return the smile. And you begin to breathe again.

We all have similar feelings. Maybe it's butterflies in your stomach, or a weakness in your knees. Whatever the precise sensation, we all know it's that unmistakable awareness that you might have just met "the one." The feeling is wonderfully intoxicating. Millions of words have been written about it and hundreds of movies have tried to capture it. We may call it that special spark of love-at-first-sight. We can call it many different things, but the bottom line is: This is your picker in action.

The process of picking is very complicated, but we are mostly unaware of it. As a biology professor, I can explain the biochemical chain reaction that occurs, producing the physiological effects. I can explain the effects of hormones and pheromones, how they produce the physiological changes such as an increased heart rate, blood pressure, and the rate of your breathing. We can talk about the dilation of your pupils and vasogestion (sexual arousal). Although this may be academically interesting, it's not very important. The essential fact is that all of these reactions start in the brain.

The picking process begins with subtle, unconscious stimuli to your brain. It is your interpretation of the stimuli that produces the response that you find so exciting. Your internal environment forms your perception of your external environment. How you interpret these cues is the important part; they tell you who you are attracted to.

I used to believe this response was fate, some supernatural phenomenon that was predetermined by the stars. I believed that there was one special person out there and it was my job to find him. I would know him by the feeling I got. That tingling, that light-headed giddiness I experienced—these were the cues telling me that my future just walked into the room.

I still believe in a "special one." But the feelings I was getting from men who turned out to be wrong for me were definitely not love. Rather, they were an indication that my picker might have been broken.

HOW CAN YOU TELL IF YOUR PICKER IS BROKEN?

If, like I used to, you have a broken picker, you get that WOW! feeling from the wrong men. The men who are available, happy, and secure do nothing for us. But the man with heartbreak written all over him (in invisible ink, of course) has us jumping around like we are walking on hot coals—and we like it. We may somehow sense that he is not good for us, but still we find ourselves compelled to pursue him, brushing

3

aside any subtle sense of warning we may occasionally feel. Like a moth to a flame, we circle. We know if we get too close we will get burned, but we are powerless to stop. The excitement of the moment is intoxicating. He has somehow set off a physical response that we interpret as love.

We become enveloped in the dream. It is like we are great writers working on a dazzling love story. All the story needs is the hero. We let out a sigh of relief as he strides into view, taller, stronger, and handsomer than all the mere mortal men around him. The point is that we are not seeing him for who he truly is. We are seeing him as we want him to be. We are blinded by our physical reactions. Because we had a certain physical response, we assume it must be love, and that *he* must be the man of our dreams.

The problem occurs when we jump into a relationship based on our emotional response without taking the time to investigate. It's almost like we have a little mental checklist. We say, "Wow, he's cute…check." "My body desires him…check." "He likes me…check. That's enough: Let's go!" And away we go, off to Heartbreak Land. And then, because we believe we have been called by fate, we may spend years trying to fix the relationship. We tell ourselves that, since our "attraction alarm" went off, he has to be "the one." After the initial excitement wears off, and things begin to go awry, we try everything we know to figure out the magical formula to make this relationship work.

I have shelves full of magazines telling me what kind of lipstick to buy and which kinds of clothes to wear. I have bought books with titles like *How to Turn Him On and Keep Him* and *How to Get Him to Marry You.* I've spent countless lonely and frustrated evenings wondering what was wrong with me. I have felt stuck and thwarted. After all, I knew from the start that he was the one, and if he would only realize it himself, we both could live happily ever after. I have believed the problem was that he just didn't understand his role. The last thing that would have occurred to me was that the relationship was doomed from the start because of my broken picker.

A broken picker is similar to a broken global positioning system (GPS) in a car. If the GPS is malfunctioning in your car, you will not arrive at the destination you seek. No matter what you do, you will end up in the wrong place. The GPS needs to be reprogrammed. Changing the "input" (such as the color of our lipstick or the way we dress, dye our hair, or prepare a romantic meal) changes nothing. Temporarily, it may appear we are heading in the right direction, but in the end we discover we are lost again. Our internal GPS (Guy Picking System) is very similar to an automotive GPS. It can malfunction, too.

HOW DO YOU KNOW FOR SURE THAT YOUR PICKER IS BROKEN?

You may suspect, if you've read this far, that your picker is broken. You can tell for sure by the men you attract and are attracted to. The men may differ physically and have other very different characteristics, but the bottom line is always the same—pain. To help you decide whether you have a broken picker that is keeping you in heartbreak instead of helping you achieve your heart's desire, please take a look at these "types" of men who attract women whose pickers are broken. Of course, these are admittedly stereotypes, and as such are generalities. They are not meant to denigrate men as a gender or as individuals. But they are offered as types, to help you examine your own experiences and relationships against them. You may recognize some of the dancers in this ballet. (And I am sure you can add some more of your own.)

I. Hit-and-Run

You can spot this type easily by the mattress that appears to be strapped to his back. He is confident and sexy and knows it. His hair is perfect, his smell alluring, and his body is rock-hard. He has the uncanny ability to sweep you off your feet...and flat onto your back. As soon as he walks into the room your knees begin to weaken. He's the one you know you should stay away from.

This is a man who loves women…he'll tell you so at every opportunity. And it's true, he does love women—he loves women the way a cat loves birds. He's Hugh Hefner personified, strutting around in his smoking jacket. You are repulsed, yet strangely attracted. You know if you get attached it will mean heartbreak, but you still find yourself compelled. You rationalize, "I'll just use HIM for sex. It will be different with me. I'm a big girl. I know what I'm doing."

Afterward, you wonder what happened. You may have been warned by your friends—you may even have been warned by *his* friends. You knew that you knew better. And yet you still wake up one day in his bed. The excitement of this type of man is fleeting. Too late you realize he was operating according to a law known only to him, one that states: Once the conquest is completed, the game is over. You end up hobbling away from this type of man feeling bruised and foolish. And him? Like the song says, he's "already gone."

2. The Teflon Don Juan

This man is the most frustrating. He appears to want a relationship, but then carefully shies away from it. His aversion is so subtle that it leaves you feeling bewildered. He just can't seem to make a relationship stick. He will commit, but for only fifteen minutes at a time.

This man is confusing because he comes on very strong at first. He starts off burning hot, showering you with attention. But just as soon as he feels he has you, his attention wanes. He becomes a phone-o-phobe. He will call you (usually at 10:30 p.m. to see if he can come over), but don't ever try to reach him. You will only get his voice mail. You're his captive, patiently (or not so patiently) waiting for him to call. He doesn't ever want to obligate himself by making plans. He says he will call you. Since he is the one you want to be with, you find yourself waiting for him…and waiting…and waiting. You spend hours wringing your hands, hoping he will call, and trying not to call him. You want to call, but you know you can't call *again*. His cell phone has probably already registered the last fifteen times you tried, and you can't bear to listen to his voice mail message one more time.

3. What Was I Thinking? (WWIT?)

You know this guy—you pull out some old school photos, and there he is, staring at you. Maybe he was dorky-looking or obviously clingy. At the time you thought he was so cute, so helpless; like a puppy. Then you woke up one day and smacked yourself on the side of the head, saying, "Oh, my God, what was I thinking?" Most likely you were not thinking. Or perhaps you interpreted his "dorkiness" or neediness as a sign that he needed you to change his life. Perhaps this man fed your illusion of your own importance. Or maybe he made you feel that somehow this relationship was going to make your life better. You ignored any signs to the contrary. We have the capacity to go to bed wildly in love, but wake up, look over, see the head on the next pillow, and scream (inwardly, of course), "WHAT WAS I THINKING?"

4. The Savior

The white knight, our savior, our knight in shining armor—there are many ways to describe this man, but the bottom line is that he has come to save us. He has come to rescue us from our dreary, tedious, mundane existence and whisk us off to Happily-Ever-After-Land. We love the Savior; he is here to provide us with much-needed shelter from a cruel and harsh world. We tend to find him charging in after a breakup or some other emotional anguish we've been through.

The Savior helps us heal; he is exactly what we need in order to recover. He provides us with warmth, protection, and comfort. He's wonderful. We love our Savior…for a time. We wish we could stay with him forever, but something happens. Slowly and subtly, our attention wanes. Where once we felt protected, we begin to feel smothered. Where once we felt comforted, we begin to feel restless, and where we once felt warm, we begin to get cold. So much perfection leaves us…bored. We start to wonder things like…is *this* it? Is this all there is? We start noticing other men and even picking fights, just to spice things up in our perfect world. Eventually we leave our Savior, sometimes in the middle of the night. Sometimes we even run away, directly to the waiting arms of his opposite.

5. The Scoundrel

This man is mysterious, exciting, and sexy as hell. There is an element of danger in being with him. Maybe he's a biker or a James Bond type. You imagine being on the back of his bike, or sitting beside him in his sports car, the wind tossing your hair, causing a rush of adrenaline. He's different, not one of those boring, everyday guys. You wouldn't find *him* in a pair of baggy shorts, cutting the grass on the weekend. No, he has more exciting things to do.

Wherever you find excitement, you will find the Scoundrel. He could be the lead singer in a band, a private investigator, or a millionaire playboy. Whatever and whoever he is, he takes your breath away. He makes you feel vulnerable, and you follow him subserviently, like a little lost puppy dog. But you soon find out he has a dark, hard, hidden coat of armor.

We wonder what happened to make him the way he is. Maybe he was hurt; maybe his mother didn't love him. We *know* there is a soft, sweet, loving man underneath that hard exterior somewhere. You tell yourself you can find him. He is just misunderstood and needs love. *Your* love. You are convinced that if you just love him enough, you (and *only* you) can melt that protective shell. So you spend the next two years beating your head against the rock wall he's constructed around his heart. He makes you crazy. He may even cause you to become obsessive, checking up on him, even stalking him. It's a long, arduous, unfulfilling, painful relationship. Finally, it ends, when he empties the bank account and runs off with a stripper. (Or worse, your best friend.)

6. Red Flag

Like a matador in a bullring who waves a red cape, the Red Flag man attracts our attention with the very thing that should repel us. Like the puzzled bull who charges toward the red cape, we race toward the Red Flag man when in reality we should run the other way. And like the bull, we don't really understand why we charge.

Just as the matador (which translates to *killer* in English, maybe appropriately in this instance) steps away at the last second, sweeping his red cape aside to reveal a deadly surprise, Red Flag man often has an unpleasant surprise in store for us. Undeterred, we regroup and charge, again and again, until, bloodied, dusty, and defeated, we are left to shake our heads as our matador, Red Flag man, leaves the ring, unscathed. The next time we see "red" we will run the other way. (Well…we at least *tell* ourselves we will.)

7. Great Potential

This is the man who is not *quite* right, but we see his potential. Maybe he drinks too much or doesn't have a job. Maybe he has a job, but he could have a better job. We tell ourselves that with our guidance we can make him better. We can teach him how to clean up after himself, we can push him to become more than he presently is. We'll use love and gentle persuasion to coax him into a better life where he will achieve his true potential.

If the gentle persuasion doesn't work, we may try manipulation or force. Sometimes we nag and pester—for his own good, of course. After all, we just want him to be the best he can be. We ignore the fact that our actions scream, "You are not acceptable as you are." He begins to resent us, resisting all our good intentions. (And after all we've done for him.) We push forward even harder, to the point of exasperation. Eventually he leaves. We are bewildered. We feel abandoned, used, and unappreciated. (We may have even put him through medical school, only to be left on the day he graduates.) We gave it all we had and got nothing in return.

He probably left us for someone "who understood him better" than we did. (Probably someone who looked up to him, giving him what he "needed to make him feel more like a man.")

Or, maybe, just maybe, we gave up on our little project and asked him to leave. We went off to find someone more appreciative of our benevolence.

8. He's a Sugar Cookie

This heartbreaker is so sweet and yummy, we could just eat him up. We look at him as if we are staring at a bakery window, wanting and salivating, imagining what it will be like when we get home with our treat. Just like a bake-shop cookie, he is delicious and satisfying for the moment, but is not good for us in the long run. The problem with the Sugar Cookie is that he doesn't reciprocate.

His love is equivalent to sweet, empty calories—nonnutritious and ultimately bad for us.

But we do love our Sugar Cookie so much, we can't believe he's just throwing us saccharine crumbs. So we make excuses for him, saying, "Oh, he's so sweet, he's just scared." Our girlfriends tell us to give him time. We fear if we push him too hard he will crumble. So we wait and hope, taking whatever little morsel he decides to mete out to us. Even if we decide we deserve more, it is difficult to let go of the allure of the Sugar Cookie.

We may decide we are going to get healthy. Yes, we are going to stop our cookie consumption and find a more nourishing diet. But when we try to leave, we go through sugar withdrawal. The obsessive thoughts begin. We forget how unhealthy our diet has been, and only remember how warm and sweet and scrumptious it was to be with our Sugar Cookie. The obsessive craving draws us back to him. The next thing we know, we are on another wild sugar binge.

And so we end up feeling fat, stupid, and ashamed of our behavior. We walk away feeling bewildered, because he looked so good, seemed so sweet. How could we have ever known he would be so bad for us? The Sugar Cookie can be the most painful of all. He can do a number on our minds, bodies, and souls. To stay healthy and fit we must stay away from those unhealthy sweets.

GNAWING ACHES

These men are all different, and your situation may be different too. But they all have one thing in common: pain—the pain of elusive and unachievable happiness. You go to bed at night with a gnawing ache that constantly questions, "Why me? What am I doing wrong?" Or you feel that piercing sting whenever you see a happy couple. You wonder what the secret is. You may even have bought a relationship self-help book— maybe a whole stack of them—in your search for answers. Maybe you even followed their advice to the letter, changing your shoes, your makeup, your toothpaste, and deodorant. Maybe you even changed what you say and how you say it. But you have still found love to be elusive.

A broken picker is frustrating. Just when you think you are on the brink of happiness, it rears its ugly head, and you are off and running, pursuing fate's latest call. Like a cruel joke, your broken picker has a way of thwarting any long-term contentment, expressing itself in a slightly different form each time. In our search to find a relationship, we may actually find someone who is willing and able to provide us with what we want—we may circumvent our broken picker and find a suitable partner once in a while. But since we still have the unresolved pain of a broken picker, we can end up sabotaging even the best relationship. We're doomed to heartbreak instead of achieving our heart's desire, as the following example demonstrates.

Yvette had been dating Steve for a few months. Things seemed to be going well, but she was becoming moody. She tried to brush off the feelings and focus on the "good stuff" about their budding relationship. A landmark birthday was coming up and she was looking forward to doing something fun. Steve asked what she would like to do, and Yvette replied that she wanted to go parasailing. She had never done it before and thought it would be exciting. What better way to celebrate this special time?

Steve had been married before, and had two children who lived in a different state. He would see his children periodically during the holidays and for one week in the summer. It just so happened that Yvette's birthday was going to fall during the week that Steve had the children with him. Steve realized that this was an important day for Yvette and wanted to do something nice—and to include everyone. Yvette had misgivings, but demurred. After all, if they were going to create a life together, as Yvette hoped, this was going to be a great opportunity for her to begin forming a relationship with his children.

As the date approached, their plans began to unravel. Steve's children didn't want to parasail; they wanted to travel down to Key West. The revised, kid-friendly plan was to leave early in the morning and drive the three hours to the Keys, spend the day jet-skiing and snorkeling, and then drive home—but Yvette really didn't want to spend most of her birthday in the car. Plus, her birthday was on a Sunday. She knew the outing would be exhausting. They'd get home late, and Yvette was dreading getting up for work on Monday morning. Her attitude was quickly becoming negative.

On Saturday night, Steve called Yvette to finalize their plans. He said his daughters wanted to ride on his motorcycle, so he was going to ride the bike while Yvette drove the truck. That was the final straw. "It's my birthday!" she thought, and she was not going to be able to do any of the things that she had wanted to do. If she went along with Steve and his children's plans, she would be spending most of the day driving, and to top it all off, he wasn't even going to be in the truck with her. She heard the words come flying out of her mouth. She wanted to take them back just as quickly as she said them, but it was too late: "I'm not going!" Alarmed and frustrated, Steve said, "Fine!" and hung up.

Yvette stared at the phone in disbelief. What just happened? She tried calling back, but only got Steve's voice mail. He had tried to deal with her growing negativity, but he had had enough. Yvette started crying to the answering machine, and begging God to allow her to take her words back. She hadn't meant it…she'd only wanted him to know she was important. Had that been so much to ask for? Eventually Steve did answer his phone; his voice was harsh and annoyed. Yvette apologized, and told him she hadn't really meant what she'd said. He relented, and they "agreed" the outing would take place as the kids and Steve had planned, and with Yvette's participation—but the damage had been done. That night Yvette tried to sleep, but spent the night crying, tossing, and turning. When morning arrived she was in no shape to go on the trip. She called Steve and declined again. She would be spending her birthday alone. Yvette's birthday was a painful example of self-sabotage.

IT'S MY PARTY AND I'LL CRY IF I WANT TO…

If Yvette's situation sounds like the ideal way to spend your birthday, please stop reading now. If you would rather drive around with a baseball bat on a Saturday night, looking for "his" car, don't continue any further. If unavailable men and obsessive relationships are your idea of a great time, please step away from this book. But if you are ready to put an end to dead-end relationships, heartaches, and misery, I've got great news for you. There's a solution, a way to jump off this merry-go-round of unfulfilling relationships. You can have the love you want. You can have a happy and healthy relationship, free from self-sabotage. There is, I assure you, a cure for a broken picker.

CHAPTER TWO

How Do You Break a Picker?

"THINGS DO NOT CHANGE; WE CHANGE."

—HENRY DAVID THOREAU

We humans are complex. We are emotional, spiritual, physical, and mental creatures. Whatever problems we have rarely have only one point of origin. Usually, there is a series of circumstances that contributes to the development of a difficulty such as a broken picker. There are four problem areas that people with broken pickers seem to have in common. Working on these will lead you out of despair and into a life you want and deserve. We will take a look at each of these troublesome areas and explain how it contributes to your having a broken picker. We will then take a look at how we can heal our pickers by taking certain steps to address these areas. The areas that lead to a broken picker are:

- Unresolved pain

- Lack of love

- Negative programming

- Not defining what you really want

UNRESOLVED PAIN

You might remember the skit by Abbott and Costello, "Who's on First?" In this classic vaudeville comedy routine, Costello is trying to figure out the names of the players on a baseball team. The problem is that the players have names like Who, What, Where, and I Don't Know. So when Costello asks the question "Who's on first?" Abbott answers,

"Yes." Costello's frustration makes for a hilarious—but for Costello, frustrating—circular conversation.

In some ways, talking about the phenomenon of a broken picker is a little like the timeless Abbott and Costello skit:

> **You:** Why do I have a broken picker?
>
> **Me:** Because you have unresolved pain.
>
> **You:** How do you know I have unresolved pain?
>
> **Me:** Because you have a broken picker.

See what I mean? When we get into a relationship or are choosing people to date, and we have unresolved pain, the pain shows itself. Think back to a time when you had hurt a part of your body; a leg, for example. If you sat down to watch TV, taking the pressure off the leg, the pain subsided. You may have reached the point at which you forgot your leg was hurt. It is only when you try to get up and use the leg that you feel the pain, reminding you that you have an injury.

The same is true for your heart. The pain makes itself known when you try to use it. When you form a relationship you make yourself vulnerable; you expose your wounded area. Whom we choose and how we act in a relationship indicates the level of pain that we have.

The pain that we feel as a result of our poor choice of men can be called *referred pain*. Referred pain is a phenomenon that occurs in the body where the pain is felt in an area different from where the actual damage is. For example, pain felt in the left shoulder and arm could very well indicate a problem with your heart. Without the accurate knowledge of referred pain, a doctor may waste precious time treating the arm. A patient could suffer damage because of this delay. Many of us are improperly diagnosing our symptoms. We are looking at the arm when our real problem is with our heart.

Our attraction to the wrong men is an indicator that a part of us needs to be healed. It is a sign that there is internal damage that needs to be addressed. If you have ever bitten the inside of your mouth, you will understand how you are strangely attracted to the very thing that brings you pain. When we have a sore spot in our mouth, our tongue naturally is attracted to that area. It is an unconscious response of the body to the pain. Over and over again, we move our tongue away from the injury, only for it to return to the damaged area the moment we stop thinking about it. Our GPS (Guy Picking System) is like that. We can try different techniques that seem to keep us away from what we know causes us pain, but they only work as long as we're concentrating on them. Then, as soon as we stop concentrating on the solution, we find ourselves unconsciously returning to the old sore spot again. It's not the men you are choosing that are the problem. It's the reason you're choosing the men you're choosing that's the problem.

It is important to understand that it's our pain that is doing the picking. It is like a child who wants attention. When children can't get positive attention, they will accept negative attention. There is a part of you that is screaming for attention, a part of you that is screaming to be healed. The more you ignore it, the more it will try to get attention any way it can.

For whatever reason—childhood abuse or trauma, past experiences, sickness, addiction, whatever—we don't trust our own deepest feelings. We usually don't trust them because when we were children, our feelings were discounted. We may have been told not to cry, or we were shamed for being scared. In some way you were taught that your feelings were unacceptable. Whatever the emotion was, it has become frozen inside us. Those frozen emotions become a part of us, causing us to be attracted to men who cause us pain, often for one reason only—because it feels familiar. When we release these old feelings, we are freed up for real love. Love is truly our heart's desire.

HUNGRY FOR LOVE

Love is one of our most basic needs. It is such a basic human requirement that an infant will die from the lack of it, the same as if it were denied food or water. (This was observed in Europe after World War II, when infants whose parents had been killed were placed in orphanages where they received clean clothing, food, and shelter, but no real love. Those who did live often grew up to exhibit extreme antisocial behaviors due to inability to love. Love is *that* important.)

When we grow up in a home that provides ample amounts of love, and we can assimilate that love into our being, we can learn to love ourselves. We have an inborn capacity and desire for love. Our experience with parental love prepares us to both give and receive love. If you come from a dysfunctional family or have a family trauma such as divorce or death, your ability to love may be affected. You may have become "love-starved," feeling like something is missing, something is wrong and you don't know what it is.

We search outside ourselves for ways to fill this love void. Besides looking for love in men, who may simply reopen the same wounds and deprivations of our early life, we may try other things, such as drugs, alcohol, shopping, and even careers. When we are love-starved, we are constantly looking for ways to fill the need; yet, paradoxically, because it's the only way we know how due to our early "conditioning," we often look for the love we crave in the same patterns of relationships that caused us to feel love-starved in the first place. We may temporarily find what passes for love in our minds, but it never seems to be either the right kind or the right amount. We need to find a source that doesn't run out. By developing self-love and trust in the universe, you never have to feel empty again. This trust in the universe begins with reprogramming your thoughts and beliefs.

NEGATIVE PROGRAMMING—REPROGRAMMING YOUR PAST

Computer programmers have a saying: "Garbage in, garbage out." It means that if initial data input is faulty, the resulting program will be faulty, too.

The same is true for us. You can't expect to be serene, confident, and contented when you are walking around all day telling yourself that the world sucks or that you can't expect any good to come from it. We may never put these feelings into actual words, or even allow ourselves to be very conscious of these thoughts. Unfortunately for many of us, the negative programming is very deep-seated, and we do an excellent job of hiding it from ourselves. It's based on old experiences and beliefs, ones that are often antiquated, incorrect, and, maybe most importantly—unconscious.

Maybe this negative programming is even based on very early misunderstandings in our lives. But for some reason we just keep replaying these negative tapes over and over in our minds, using them as guidelines even when we know they cause us pain. These are the voices that you hear throughout your day, the words spoken by your mom, your dad, your third-grade teacher, the bully down the block, or even someone else whom you may have loved—or feared or hated—very deeply. These are the voices that trip us up.

These are the voices that have us quitting before we even try.

My self-defeating beliefs are based on the things I tell myself. My soul's core belief in the dating situation is that I am not good enough to be in the presence of this talented and gorgeous man (whoever he may be). But why would I feel this way? Poor programming. If our home lives were loving and nurturing all the time, so would be the voices we hear from within. But if they weren't loving and nurturing (and very few of our home lives were paragons of constant love and nurturance), then the voices we hear within us would reflect that. Since no one is born and raised under perfect conditions, we all have "corrupt programs"—programs that we need to erase and rewrite, in computer parlance.

NOT DEFINING WHAT YOU WANT

How many times have people asked you, "What would you like?"
And how many times have you thought, "I don't know. What are my
options?" So many times we don't stop to think about what we really
want; instead we wait for someone to offer choices among which we
can decide.

When I was in high school, I was asked to decide what I wanted to do
with my life. Did I want to go to college, go to trade school, or get a job?
I decided I wanted to go to college, but I wasn't really sure what to major
in. I knew I loved animals and I thought I might like to be a veterinarian
or at least a veterinary technician. But instead of looking at schools that
offered programs that would qualify me for such professions, I chose
a local school and decided to take what they had to offer—because
although I knew I wanted to go to college, I didn't want to be too far
from my boyfriend. (In case you are wondering, yes, this was the man
who would one day jump on the hood of my car with the distributor
wires he'd yanked from the engine.) I chose a school that was only about
an hour away so I could come home on weekends to be with him.
However, this school didn't have any programs in veterinary science.
They did have a program called "animal husbandry." I said, "Close
enough," and applied.

I was accepted, and soon I was getting ready to go off to college. Not
long before I was ready to go, I received a letter from the school.
"Congratulations on your admission. We only have one other question
to complete your enrollment. Please choose from the following list which
animals you would like to study: horse or cow." I was a suburbanite
with no experience with either animal. I had to decide what I wanted to
spend the next several years of my life studying. I had never been on a
horse, and the closest I had been to a cow was working at McDonald's.
After careful consideration, I chose the horse, because it seemed more
sophisticated than a cow.

And so I spent a lot of time and money studying something I had no interest in because I never took the time to define exactly what I wanted (and because I allowed my decision to be influenced by my need for love, rather than by my true career interests). As the old saying goes, "If you keep doing what you're doing, you'll keep getting what you're getting." What I discovered, after years of making most of my life choices pretty much the same way, was that the same principles that applied to my college education and early career choices also apply to my relationships. If I don't take the time to define what I really want, and allow extraneous factors to influence my decision, I can easily end up wasting a lot of time with something (or someone) not quite right.

If you are tired of "getting what you've been getting," this book will help you change what you are doing. Let's take a look at fixing your picker, and moving you further away from heartbreak and closer to your heart's desire.

CHAPTER THREE

Healing Your Picker, Step by Step

"YOU CAN NEVER PLAN THE FUTURE BY THE PAST."

—EDMUND BURKE

I once brought my vehicle to the tire store. My old tires had worn out very quickly, and I was upset. I told the man at the counter that I was never going back to the old store where I'd bought the tires because they were terrible. I showed him my car, pointed at the tires, and said, "See? I just got those a few months ago." The attendant was very nice and gentle as he pointed out my problem. "It's not the tires that are the problem," explained. "It's your car's alignment. It's way off. I can install new tires for you, but you will be in the same place as you are now in just a few months. Or I can take your car in, do some work to correctly align the car, and then put on new tires. They will last for 35,000 miles." Our lives work the same way.

Trying to make changes anywhere in our lives without doing the realignment work is just going to get us more of what we've been getting all along. Healing a broken picker takes some time and some work, but there's no other way to get the true, long-term results you desire.

STEP BY STEP

This book contains activities designed to fix your picker. It consists of twelve steps or actions. It's not a twelve-step program like Alcoholics Anonymous or Narcotics Anonymous. But if you are in a twelve-step program you will be familiar with the idea. I had been working the Twelve Steps in my own recovery for more than seventeen years when I came to the point in my recovery where I realized I needed to do this work. In fact, it was in the rooms of recovery that I first heard the term "broken picker."

It is no coincidence that there are twelve steps or activities. The number twelve is one of those numbers that are meaningful. In numerology, twelve is considered to be the number that forms a complete and perfect harmonious unit. And in spirituality, the number twelve signifies faith and all the aspects of love. In fact, there are twelve aspects of love:

- ♥ respect
- ♥ compassion
- ♥ gratitude
- ♥ truth
- ♥ reverence
- ♥ open-mindedness
- ♥ discipline
- ♥ faith
- ♥ generosity
- ♥ oneness
- ♥ selflessness
- ♥ detachment (freedom/serenity)

What more perfect number could there be for fixing your picker?

The time frame of twelve weeks (give or take) is used because, just as when I needed my tires realigned, work takes time. The activities in this book are about making changes. Most of us are resistant to change; that's only human. We may have great intentions when we begin a healthy practice, only to find, in short order, we are back to our old routines. But the twelve-week time frame isn't cast in stone. The actual time you take to complete the steps will depend on where you are in the process when you start out. You'll modify the program to meet your particular needs.

These twelve steps are designed to address the specific conditions that heal a broken picker. Each action has a specific goal in mind that addresses the different factors that contribute to a broken picker. As you go along with the exercises, I'll explain why each action is important and how to perform the action, and suggest how long to continue performing it. Effective "picker alignment" is a multilayered process designed to help you develop self-love and improve self-esteem, release and heal old pain, reprogram negative thought patterns, grow spiritually, and finally, discover your true heart's desires.

CHAPTER FOUR

Step One

Personal Retreat

"IF THERE WERE NO CHANGE,
THERE WOULD BE NO BUTTERFLIES."

—AUTHOR UNKNOWN

*T*ime heals all wounds (it may also be true that, in the words of the old saying, "time wounds all heels"). It's trite, but true, and healing a broken picker is no different from any other kind of healing. It takes time. Of course, being human, we all wish that the instant we realize our brokenness, our woundedness, we can heal instantly. But it doesn't work that way. To heal a broken picker we need time, and sometimes we need to take a step back, not to isolate, but to protect ourselves and give ourselves a chance for healing to take place. Sometimes, in order to advance, we need to take a retreat. A personal retreat, that is.

WHAT IS A PERSONAL RETREAT?

A personal retreat is one in which you take time for yourself. You already know that in order to love another person you must first love yourself. But what does love really mean? What does it mean when you hear "He loves his car" or "She loves her garden" or "They love their family"? It usually means that they spend time with the object of that "love." He spends time cleaning his car, she spends time tending her garden, they spend time with their family.

That's what a personal retreat is about; it's about time spent loving yourself. You are loving yourself when you give yourself time just for you. You are giving yourself time to do the activities in this book, time to heal and grow, and time to decide what you want from life. By taking a personal retreat, you are making a commitment to yourself and taking a very important step along the path of self-love.

A retreat can be defined as a period of withdrawal for prayer, meditation, study, or instruction. But what are you withdrawing from? In the context of our present discussion, you are withdrawing from male attention. You will take a break from dating. You will stop dating men and start dating yourself. You are going to be taking the time to get to know yourself better.

WHY DO I NEED A PERSONAL RETREAT?

There are several reasons to participate in a personal retreat. Three of the biggest reasons are:

1. It's harder to solve a problem when you are in the middle of it;

2. You need time for yourself; and

3. You need time to heal.

It is quite difficult to solve a problem when you are in the middle of it. The solution to any problem often becomes apparent only after you stop frantically searching for it. Our frenzied efforts to solve a problem can actually become a barrier to its solution, or may even add to the problem. The guidance we need becomes apparent once we stop focusing on our difficulty.

This can be illustrated by a simple example. Think back to a time when you were trying to remember something—maybe a person's name or the name of a place. The more you focused on it, the more frustrated you became. But as soon as you let go and turned your attention somewhere else, the name popped into your head. The same principle applies to a personal retreat. We can't expect to find an answer to our relationship problem while we are in the center of it. When we remove ourselves and focus on something else, the solution becomes evident.

You need to take this time and focus on you and become comfortable with yourself. This is one of life's ironies: You will never be happy in a relationship until you are able to be happy without one.

In the past, when I felt lonely I would look to men as a source of comfort. I would look to them to make me feel good about myself. When I was getting attention from a man, I felt beautiful and wanted. But if I wasn't getting attention I felt undesirable. My moods fluctuated, depending on how much attention I felt I needed and was getting. This was never an enjoyable place to be. I had trouble being comfortable with myself.

This feeling of being uncomfortable in my own skin made intimacy difficult. I would get into a relationship with a man and expect him to make me feel lovable. When he didn't, I would try to get the attention that I felt I was lacking. Often, I would act out by trying to attract the attention of other men. This caused difficulties in my primary relationship. My partner justifiably felt uneasy about my commitment to him and questioned my ability to be faithful. My own insecurity and lack of self-worth caused him to be unsure and pull back. I was creating a vicious cycle that always ended in heartache.

One of the main reasons I felt so uncomfortable with myself was that I had never taken time to grieve and heal from past hurts. My past relationship patterns were to jump from one relationship to the next. I didn't want to feel the ache of grieving, so in order to avoid the pain I'd focus on the excitement of a new relationship. Unfortunately, this created more unresolved pain that needed to be released. What I discovered was that my fear of the pain was much greater than the pain itself. By taking time for a personal retreat, and using that time to release that old unresolved pain, I was preparing myself for a much healthier relationship.

RETREAT!

While I was writing this book, my friend Lindsay called to tell me some big news.

"I'm moving out!" she said.

"What happened?"

As she told me of her dawning realization that her partner was not "the one," I began to think she might be a prime candidate for a personal retreat. She could even serve as a research subject, if she would agree.

I explained about the book I was writing, told her about the twelve-step plan for healing her broken picker, and asked if she'd give it a try.

"Yeah," she said. "I'd love that."

"It has different activities designed to help you heal and figure out what you really want."

"It sounds like exactly what I need, and I'll have plenty of free time now that I am moving out."

"I'll send you a copy."

"Okay, I'll start right away."

"The first thing you do is called a personal retreat."

"Cool, sounds like fun. What is it?"

"It is where you take a break from dating to figure out what you want."

"Do you mean I can't date?"

"Well…yes."

"Oh, you don't understand. I'm thirty-six years old and I want to have children. I can't afford to take time off from dating."

"Wait, didn't you just tell me you haven't moved out yet?"

"Yes."

"Are you planning to take any time off to heal and figure out what you want?"

"Oh, yes, but I am still going to date. In fact, I am already talking to someone."

She was talking to this new potential lover while she was still living with someone else. In two years I will probably get exactly the same phone call from her—only then she will be two years older and feeling even more pressure. She doesn't realize that anyone she meets right now will bring up the same issues. By jumping into another relationship, my friend is not solving her problem, because her thinking hasn't changed. She is just delaying her healing. She doesn't realize that the reason she is in a hurry to meet and mate with the right man is precisely the reason she needs to take the time to do the activities in the book. She is right in thinking she doesn't have time to waste. But she needs to use the time she has in order to heal, to improve her self-esteem and change her self-talk, to figure out what she really wants in a relationship, and then to take the time to find it. Then, and only then, will she be ready to attract her heart's desire. Unfortunately, she will probably find herself bewildered, always wondering why she can't seem to find or attract the right guy. Little does she know that the right guy is already out there getting ready for her—if she would only take the time to get ready for him.

In her book *Facing Love Addiction*, Pia Mellody explains that until we "acquire more healthy ways of thinking, feeling, and behaving in a relationship healthy people will continue to appear less attractive. Just changing partners to a healthier person without doing the work of recovery will not solve the problem." (*Facing Love Addiction: Giving Yourself the Power to Change the Way You Love*. Pia Mellody, Andrea Wells Miller, and J. Keith Miller. © 2003, HarperCollins.)

HOW LONG SHOULD I STAY ON MY PERSONAL RETREAT?

Each personal retreat will be different. How long will it take? The length of time will depend on where you are in your journey. Some retreats may be as short as a few weeks, while others may last ninety days or more. Here are some guidelines to help you decide how much time you want yours to take:

- If you haven't just exited a relationship, then all you need to do is give yourself the time to do the steps in this book. This could be as short as a week, but I would recommend thirty days.

- If you were recently in a relationship and it ended more than a month ago, then a sixty-day retreat is recommended. This will give you time to do the work in the book, while also providing you with important time to grieve the breakup of the relationship.

- If you are still in a relationship that isn't a happy one for you, or you are just ending it, then a ninety-day retreat is recommended. You need this time to grieve and heal. Just as a broken arm needs a certain amount of time to heal, so does your heart.

If you are not sure where to begin, start with a sixty-day hiatus. If this seems too extreme, it may be easier to commit if you start with a thirty-day sabbatical. If Lindsay had taken a ninety-day personal retreat two years before that phone call instead of jumping into the relationship she was looking to end on the day she called me, she might now be making the decisions about marriage and motherhood she wanted, rather than looking for a new place to live.

MY PERSONAL RETREAT HESITATION

I confess that the first time my mentor suggested a personal retreat, I was resistant. I was unhappy and frustrated with my on-again, off-again relationship, but I was reluctant to take a break. I began my first retreat halfheartedly and wasn't really being honest with myself. In the back of my mind, I was still manipulating. I was hoping that if my boyfriend realized I was gone, he would miss me so much that he would come back and commit to our relationship, and everything would be fine. I had read somewhere that if you stop seeing a man and he comes back in sixty days, then he is serious. So I did the retreat for sixty days. I just knew that he would come back. Then I could stop this silly thing and get on with my life.

And guess what? In sixty days he did come back. I was overjoyed. But I was not the pushover he had left behind. In those sixty days I had begun the process of valuing myself. So, when he returned and tried to fall into bed with me, as we'd done so many times before, a little part of me resisted. I was tired of him coming and going, leaving me feeling used. I wanted a relationship, not casual sex. So this time I did something different: I asked for what I wanted. I told him I wanted an exclusive relationship with him before we had sex again.

To my surprise, he was not upset. He was a gentleman, and said he respected my wishes. He smiled and seemed proud of me. I was elated. He did not say he would give me a commitment, but said he would go home and think about it. In the days that followed we had several dates. He wanted to have sex, but I stuck to my guns and restated my desire for a commitment. Each time he would respect me and go home. He became more attentive. He started calling every day, just to talk. We dated for several more weeks, and I was excited that my plan seemed to be working.

Then, one day, his calls stopped. After three long, agonizing days, he called. He told me that he had been thinking about what I wanted, and decided he could not give it to me. I was devastated. My first reaction was to say, "Okay, never mind. I will take whatever you have to offer me, just don't leave me." But I didn't. I wanted more, and I was finally realizing I was worth it. I was no longer willing to settle for love scraps. I had to let him go. I was now truly ready for my personal retreat.

PACKING FOR YOUR PERSONAL RETREAT

To get the benefits from your personal retreat you need a complete break from men; call it a man-ban, a date-break, or a "he-tox." Whatever you would like to call it, the bottom line is…NO MEN. No dating, no phone calls, no emails, and, of course, no sexual contact with anyone. Start by deleting the men's numbers from your cell phone or phone book. If a man is a friend whom you may want to call after you've completed your retreat, then write his number down for later. Put the paper somewhere safe, or give it to a woman friend to hold for you. Next, remove all the men's email addresses from your online address book. If you have a little black book, burn it.

Tell all your guy pals what you are doing and explain that you won't be able to talk with them for a while. If they are your true friends, they will understand and support you. If they don't support you, then you are better off without them.

Stop all behavior that gets you attention from men. Yes, that even means that cute delivery guy. Order from a different restaurant. Avoid places where men hang out…no sports bars or tractor-pulls. If you are invited to a place where there are a lot of singles, don't go. It may seem like a big sacrifice, but it's only temporary. (Don't worry, you will not forget how to date.) Go see a movie with a girlfriend instead. But skip the love stories; they will only make you miss the male attention you see onscreen.

Put all your sexy clothes in a box. Sleep in those old comfy pajamas you wouldn't want a man to see you in. If you've been driving by a construction area where you've been getting wolf whistles on the way to work, change your route. Go to the gym on off-hours or take the female-dominated classes. Do not go anywhere you know you will see men whose attention you might be even remotely interested in.

You may meet someone and be tempted to be diverted. This is normal. There's always a part of us that resists anything new or unfamiliar. It is almost as if your resolve is being tested. Are you really committed to your heart's desires? If you answer yes, you will continue along the path you've now begun. You've heard the saying, "no pain, no gain"? A little work (a little pain) will garner you a little gain. A lot of work/pain will get you a lot of gain. You get to choose.

To help me stay committed to my decision, I announced my intentions to all my friends. I told them what I was doing and why. To my surprise, everyone was supportive, and even offered to help. A few of my girlfriends said they were going to watch me, and if my retreat worked for me, they would try it for themselves.

Some days were tough. When I felt down, I would want to call or email a guy. On those days, I wanted to give up. I told myself ninety days was too long. But I'd made a commitment to myself. So, on the days when I felt particularly challenged, I would take a "one day at a time" approach. Just for that one day, I told myself, I would not call a guy. I told myself, I don't know what I will do tomorrow, but I definitely won't call today. Instead of calling a guy, I would call a girlfriend who was supportive and talk to her.

I recommend asking a girlfriend to be your "retreat buddy." Explain to her what you are doing and why. Ask her if it would be okay if you call her when you feel yourself weakening and wanting to call a man. I think you'll find that most friends will be honored to help you in this way.

Stopping any behavior that is familiar to you, particularly behavior that you've used to release tension or make yourself feel better, even temporarily, is difficult. Being accustomed to a situation, even a painful one, promises a certain level of comfort. Change takes courage and usually requires support from others. But, most of all, it takes faith that the change you're working to achieve will benefit you. Sometimes the pain needs to become worse before it gets better. Remind yourself of this whenever you need courage.

LIFTOFF

When we're breaking old habits or starting anything new, it takes a lot of effort in the beginning—just like the energy needed to launch a rocket. Once it's in orbit, gravity will become its ally, but before that happens, gravity is the enemy. Enormous amounts of energy must be expended during liftoff in order to counteract its effects. The beginning of your retreat may be like this. Remind yourself often that you are taking the time to go on this retreat because you want and deserve a loving, committed relationship. Consider putting up a few sticky notes to refresh your memory. This retreat is only temporary, and the benefits will be for a lifetime. Meanwhile, the time will go fast.

Taking this time is essential. This is the first step of a process that will lead you to the love and life you want. Seneca, the Roman philosopher, said it best: "It is not because things are difficult that we do not dare; it is because we do not dare that things are difficult."

Activity

- Implement a personal retreat.

- Copy, print, sign, and post in a conspicuous place the Personal Retreat Agreement form on page 39.

- Delete men from your phone and computer.

- Avoid areas where men congregate.

- Avoid wearing clothing that will tend to attract male attention.

- Get a retreat buddy.

Personal Retreat Agreement

I, _____, AM MAKING A COMMITMENT
(YOUR NAME)

TO A _____-DAY PERSONAL RETREAT.
(NUMBER)

BY SIGNING THIS AGREEMENT, I AM GIVING MYSELF THE
GIFT OF TIME TO WORK ON MYSELF. I AM MAKING THIS
PROMISE SO I HAVE TIME TO HEAL, GROW, AND DISCOVER
MY TRUE HEART'S DESIRE. DURING MY RETREAT:

I WILL DELETE FROM MY PHONE ALL NUMBERS
OF MEN TO WHOM I HAVE LOOKED FOR ATTENTION.

I WILL AVOID SEEKING ATTENTION
FROM MEN ONLINE AND IN PERSON.

I WILL NOT DO ANYTHING TO PUT MYSELF IN A
POSITION TO BE TEMPTED TO BREAK THIS AGREEMENT.

I AM COMMITTED TO A BETTER LIFE.

I WILL CALL _____ INSTEAD OF CALLING A MAN.
(NAME OF RETREAT BUDDY)

I WILL LIMIT MY CONTACT WITH ANYONE
WHO DOESN'T SUPPORT MY COMMITMENT.

I WILL NOT WEAR ATTENTION-SEEKING CLOTHES.

I WILL AVOID AREAS AND OCCASIONS WHERE
THERE WILL BE MEN NOT RELATED TO ME.

I AM MAKING THIS PROMISE TO
TRANSFORM MY LIFE FROM ONE OF HEARTBREAK
TO ONE IN WHICH I FIND MY HEART'S DESIRE.

CHAPTER FIVE

Step Two

Taking Care of Yourself

"HE WHO HAS HEALTH HAS HOPE;
AND HE WHO HAS HOPE HAS EVERYTHING."

—ARABIAN PROVERB

THE GRAY DOG

My friend Bill decided to buy a prizewinning Weimaraner. The dog was a handsome gray male that Bill was planning to breed. One day Bill and I went out for a drive with the dog. Normally Bill's driving is rather aggressive, fast, with jackrabbit starts and rolling "stops" at stop signs. But this trip was different. During this drive, Bill drove at the speed limit, accelerated gradually, came to complete stops at stop signs, and even looked both ways before proceeding. Surprised by the sudden change, I remarked, "Bill, your driving has really improved."

He said, "It's the dog. Not only has my driving changed; now, I get up early to exercise him. I prepare him a special nutritious diet. I make sure there is no noise in the house after 10 p.m., and I even stopped smoking in the house."

I thought, "Wow, he does all that for a dog, but for himself, he stays out late drinking and smoking, eats junk food, and never gets exercise." As I was thinking this, I looked at him. He said, "What?"

I said, "If only we treated ourselves like prizewinning Weimaraners!"

TREATING MYSELF LIKE BEST IN SHOW OR A SCRAPPY SHELTER POOCH?

For years, I took care of myself like Bill did before the Weimaraner. I took little thought when it came to food. I had a busy life that left little time to prepare meals. I grabbed whatever was available, usually junk food, when I became hungry. I would tell myself, "It's okay, I'll eat better next time," or "I've been good, I can afford this," before chowing down on something I'd later regret. I would often graze on snacks all day, and then go home at night ravenous. I would end up eating a big meal right before bed.

I was frustrated because I was gaining weight, but it didn't seem like I was eating *that* much. I skipped breakfast to conserve calories, not realizing that my body was responding to the calorie restriction as if I were starving and, as a way of storing reserves, was slowing my metabolism. The next time I ate, I ate fewer calories, and as a result, more calories would be placed in fat storage on my hips and buttocks, thereby adding to my growing weight problem.

I felt listless most of the time. By mid-afternoon my energy level would crash. I drank a caffeinated drink to revive myself. Unfortunately, the caffeine made me irritable and made it more difficult for me to fall asleep at night. I would stay up late, not getting my needed eight hours of sleep, making me tired the next day. I started the day with more caffeine, which caused me to crash again in the afternoon, when I'd begin repeating this endless cycle of fatigue, irritability, sleeplessness, and weight gain. (I was *so-o-o-o-o* much fun to be around!)

I finally made some incremental changes to improve my life and health. I started losing weight; I looked and felt better, and I became more productive at work. As my health improved, so did my attitude and my relationships. I needed to start treating myself like Best in Show if I wanted men to treat me like I had a pedigree.

WHY IS A GOOD DIET IMPORTANT?

Your diet provides you with the raw materials that build your body. Though we all know this intellectually, I suggest that, while you're on your personal retreat, you etch this point into your mind with a metaphor. Let's suppose you are building a house. You decide to use inferior materials because they are cheaper and easier to find. Your neighbor decides to build the identical house, but he chooses the best materials available. Which house do you believe will last longer and have lower maintenance costs? The answer, of course, is the one made with the better materials. Which one would you want to live in?

Your body is similar to those houses. Just as with those structures, you may not see the effects of poor materials for several years. Bad habits that you were able to get away with when you were young begin to cause you problems as you get older.

Sometimes the consequences of building with poor materials do not make themselves apparent until after a major event such as a hurricane. People, too, may get along fine for many years, then encounter an event where they pay the price for using those poor materials.

To have the best structure, you need proper materials as well as a good maintenance program, and that means eating right and choosing the best types of foods possible. Along with good food choices, good maintenance also involves exercise. The faculty at the Department of Nutrition at the Harvard School of Public Health has redesigned the old food pyramid. The new food pyramid not only shows what foods to eat; it also contains exercise as a key ingredient. The new pyramid is based on the fact that the most important determinants of good health are what we eat and how active we are.

EATING RIGHT

Some tips for eating right include:

- Choose good carbs, not no carbs. Whole grains are the best if you're eating breads or rolls.

- Fish, poultry, nuts, and beans are the best choices for protein. Avoid red meats that have high fat content.

- Choose healthy fats, limit saturated fats, and avoid trans fats. Plant oils, nuts, and fish are the healthiest sources.

- Choose a fiber-filled diet, rich in whole grains, vegetables, and fruits.

- Eat more vegetables and fruits. Go for color and variety—dark green, yellow, orange, and red.

- Get calcium, but choose more nondairy sources such as leafy green vegetables, beans, and tofu.

- Take a good-quality multivitamin daily.

EXERCISE

Exercise is the best thing you can do to improve your health, take care of yourself, and begin the process of healing your picker. Exercise will help keep diseases like diabetes, cancer, heart disease, and osteoporosis at bay. Exercise not only makes you look better; it can make you feel better, improve your mood, and reduce the effects of aging.

TYPES OF EXERCISE

There are two types of exercise, aerobic and anaerobic. Aerobic literally means "with oxygen." Your body needs oxygen to burn calories. By increasing your heart rate you burn more calories, which is evident by your increased breathing rate. Because it increases your heart rate, aerobic exercise is also called cardiovascular exercise, or "cardio." These exercises include activities such as walking, jogging, swimming, and dancing.

Anaerobic means "without oxygen." These types of exercises do not tend to increase your heart rate, but are important to maintain muscle tone and strength. They include such activities as yoga, stretching, and weight training.

Both forms of exercise are important and have different benefits.

IMPROVE YOUR MOOD

As you exercise, you produce chemicals called endorphins. One class of endorphins is called opioids. When secreted, opioids have a euphoric effect. They can block pain signals and produce feelings of pleasure, which are responsible for the "runner's high," or that feeling of well-being during and following an intense workout.

Not only do these naturally occurring opioids give you a better mental outlook; they elevate growth hormones. There is evidence that growth hormones can improve mood and motivation, ward off the signs of aging by increasing bone and muscle mass, bolster the heart's ability to contract, and decrease body fat. Jack LaLanne, the fitness guru, is ninety-five. He continues to work out every morning. He is the poster child for vitality, looking more like a man in his fifties than in his nineties.

Developing a routine aerobic exercise schedule is important. (No personal retreat would be complete without it.) It is also important to add anaerobic activities to your exercise regimen.

MUSCLES BURN MORE CALORIES

Ever notice with annoyance that men are able to shed weight more easily than women when on a diet? That's due to several factors, including hormonal differences, but one big factor is that men have more muscle mass than women—and muscle burns more calories just by virtue of being muscle. Women have to work a little harder to lose weight through dieting, and exercise that builds muscle can help you achieve the weight loss you want. Not only do you burn more calories while you exercise; a fit body also burns more calories at rest. Toned muscles simply burn more calories, whether active or at rest. The VO_{2max} is the maximum capacity of an individual's body to transport and utilize oxygen during incremental exercise and is a measure of fitness. It can be twice as great in a trained endurance athlete than in an untrained person. This indicates that the toned muscle will burn more calories than the out-of-shape muscle, even though the movement is the same. This fact will help you look better and feel better sooner, as you continue with your incrementally increasing exercise. What a healing gift to give yourself. (Don't worry about spoiling your curves with too much muscle; your female hormones will not allow you to bulk up like a champion weightlifter unless you go in for serious bodybuilding.)

HOW TO EXERCISE

People often begin an exercise regime with high expectations or unrealistic goals. They may want to lose thirty pounds in thirty days, or they may decide to work out for two hours a day right off the bat. Often, this overzealous behavior results in exhaustion, injury, and disappointments. You can end up dropping the entire idea of getting more exercise because of poor methodology. You don't want to get caught in that trap. Use this personal retreat time to explore programs that will work well for you.

Instead of an overly optimistic exercise plan, begin with small, incremental changes. In fact, you don't have to "exercise" at all. Just making small changes to your physical activities during the course of a day can make big improvements. These activities can include taking the stairs instead of the elevator at work, parking at the far end of the parking lot and walking, or doing an activity such as walking, working out on a treadmill or bike, or going to the gym one night a week instead of watching television. How about going for a nice stroll after dinner or a Saturday afternoon bike ride? Just getting up and moving is an improvement over couch-potato habits.

If you decide to incorporate a more formal exercise regime, I would encourage and applaud you. If you have been thinking about joining a gym, then please do so. The ideal goal suggested by the National Institutes of Health is thirty minutes of aerobic exercise every day. You can start slowly and work your way up to thirty minutes per day.

Mix up your activities and try different things. This helps keep you interested and motivated. Don't be like the man who decided he couldn't exercise at all because his exercise bike had a flat tire. Do what you can, listen to your body, and make sure you get enough rest. Exercise will also help you sleep better.

SLEEP

As of this writing, approximately seventy million people in the United States are affected by a sleep problem. About forty million Americans suffer from chronic sleep disorders, and an additional twenty to thirty million are affected by intermittent sleep-related problems. (National Commission on Sleep Disorders Research, 1992)

WHY IS SLEEP SO IMPORTANT?

A 1996 study by the University of Chicago Medical Center showed that sleep deprivation severely affects the human body's ability to metabolize glucose, which can lead to early-stage type 2 diabetes. In addition, several studies indicate that there is a correlation between decreased hours of sleep and increased obesity.

A 2008 research project at the University of Chicago's medical school kept young, healthy volunteers awake all but four hours a night for six nights running. The result: The levels of the subjects' hormones shifted. There was an increase in a hormone called leptin that affects appetite. They became ravenously hungry, wolfing down pizza and ice cream long after they would normally have felt full, and their blood sugar shot up to prediabetic levels—an ominous result after less than one week of inadequate sleep.

People who do not get enough sleep are prone to more aggressive behavior, are more stressed, and tend to be more irritable than people who do get sufficient sleep. Prolonged sleep deprivation has even been fatal to experimental animals. Sleep deprivation has long been used as an interrogation technique or a form of torture.

HOW MUCH DO YOU NEED?

There is no clear consensus regarding how much sleep is enough. However, researchers have found that less than six hours a night can impair reaction time, judgment, memory, motivation, and patience. The amount needed for each person is different, and it changes during your life (as you have probably learned).

Experts agree that seven to eight hours of sleep are required for high achievement. If you fail to get at least seven nightly hours, you are probably operating at a cognitive disadvantage. New scientific research shows that going without enough sleep for more than an occasional day or two can wreak havoc on your health, memory, concentration, mood, and ability to make decisions—even if you think you are doing fine.

One experiment at the University of Pennsylvania medical school kept subjects up until 4 a.m., woke them at 8 a.m., and then gave them a series of tests designed to measure memory, alertness, and the ability to react quickly to new information. The researchers were startled to find that subjects' mental acuity declined markedly after just one night and kept dropping with each successive night of four hours' sleep. Even more worrying: The study's volunteers were unaware of their impairment. One woman, so fatigued that she could barely say her name, was nonetheless certain she was capable of driving herself home. Those running the project observed that, like drunk drivers, those suffering the effects of sleep deprivation had no idea how impaired they actually were.

HOW DO YOU GET A GOOD NIGHT'S SLEEP?

The US National Institutes of Health offers tips for getting a good night's sleep:

- ❤ Stick to a regular sleep schedule.

- ❤ Avoid exercising fewer than five or six hours before bedtime.

- ❤ Avoid caffeine, nicotine, and/or alcohol before bed.

- ❤ Avoid large meals and beverages late at night.

- ❤ Don't take naps after 3 p.m.

- ❤ Relax before bed, taking time to unwind with a hot bath, a good book, or soothing music.

- ❤ If you're still awake after more than twenty minutes in bed, get up and do something relaxing until you feel sleepy. Anxiety over not being able to sleep can make it harder to fall asleep.

When I go through a tough time or am processing something emotionally or mentally, I sometimes wake up in the middle of the night and am unable to go back to sleep. I've found this to be a perfect time to journal (see Chapter 7, "Journaling"). I use this time to write about whatever is bothering me or to write down whatever thoughts are keeping me awake. The great part about this is that I often discover that once I've written down whatever is on my mind, I don't have to keep thinking about it. I don't have to remember it or figure it out. It is safely written in my journal, so I am free to think about something else (or, better yet, nothing at all). Once I have written my thoughts in my journal, I find I'm able to drift off to sleep quickly. Try it; you may be pleasantly surprised.

However, if you are still unable to sleep after journaling, then get up. Do something. Just make sure you don't have to think very much about whatever you're doing. Reorganize your sock drawer. Dust. Do anything that you can do mindlessly. Read a boring book. Do not read a suspense novel because that will surely keep you up longer. Pull out an old biology textbook and start reading. (If my former students are any indication, that should have you back asleep in a few minutes.)

Good-quality sleep, plenty of exercise, and eating right are important for building good health. You are getting ready not just for the next phase of your life, but also to enjoy your life more. This begins with taking better care of yourself. When I am having trouble with motivation, I remind myself that living a healthy lifestyle may not only add years to my life; it may make those years worth living.

Activity:

- Choose healthy foods and take a good-quality vitamin/mineral supplement daily.

- Make sure you have printed a copy of the Personal Retreat Agreement on page 39. Sign it and place it where you will see it every day.

- Get more physical exercise.

- Sleep at least six hours a night.

THE
WHOLE
YOU

CHAPTER SIX

Step Three
Meditation:
Getting Grounded

"SERVE, LOVE, MEDITATE, REALIZE."

—THE FOUR PRINCIPLES OF YOGA

*F*or years people had suggested that I try meditation. I *had* tried it, many times, but always gave up, frustrated by the noise in my head. Sitting down and trying to be still would make me uncomfortable. With a million things running through my head, I would become anxious. My mind would throw things at me like "You are wasting time," "I think you left the iron on," or "You need to call the cable guy now." Eventually I would give up, convinced that meditation didn't work for me.

It would take a while for me to realize what was causing my discomfort. But until I did realize what was making me uncomfortable, I stuck with it, and by continuing to practice meditation, even though I felt uncomfortable, the noisy static that would not let me hear the silence inside me began to diminish. Slowly, I became able to ignore the urgent thoughts that wanted me to stop meditating. I was finally able to hear the small voice that I had been running from most of my life. I heard those words that I was terrified of hearing. This was the voice that I had tried to drown with alcohol or food or to run away from with activities and distractions. I heard the voice of the part of me that kept picking the wrong men. At last, I stopped running.

WHAT IS MEDITATION?

Meditation is a discipline in which the mind is focused on an object of thought or awareness. It usually involves turning your attention to a single point of reference. Meditation is recognized as a component of almost all religions and has been practiced for more than five thousand years. Hindu philosophy uses several different types of yoga meditation. Kabbalah in Judaism is a meditative field of study, and the Catholic Christian practice of saying the rosary has been compared to Eastern meditation, which focuses the mind on an individual object. Prayer and meditation are slightly different but can be used together. It's been said that prayer is talking to God, whereas meditation is listening.

I began with a form of Buddhist meditation. Buddhists believe that meditation will lead toward enlightenment or spiritual awakening, and a peace of the mind believed to be the fundamental nature of the mind, which can be reached once it is free of afflictive states such as cravings, anger, and depression. These afflictive states are believed to be the root cause of human suffering. *Nirvana* can be translated as "blowing out," as one does a candle. When the afflictive states of craving, anger, depression, and the like are "blown out" through the practice of meditation and right living, a person may be said to have reached *nirvana*, which is not a place, but a state of being.

Meditation is simply the act of slowing down enough to allow all those feelings you have been hiding from to bubble up. We all have thoughts and feelings we don't like. But instead of feeling them and letting them go, we continually stuff them down. This causes us problems, or, as the Buddhist believes, this stuffing down of our thoughts and feelings causes our suffering. The act of meditation allows the feelings to come to the surface, where you are free to deal with them and let them go. The problem many of us have is that ordinarily we begin to feel the emotion and then push it back down. It comes up later, and we push it down again. Each time it is pushed down, it is buried more deeply; but the place within ourselves where we bury it, hidden deep within our outer being, only provides the soil where our discomfort with the thought or feeling grows.

Just like me, many of us start to feel uncomfortable when beginning meditation, and instead of facing the feelings that may come up, we reject the practice of meditation. But if we want a life of bliss, we can't continue to run away from our feelings.

I realize now that many of my addictive behaviors are the result of my attempts to push down or cover up my pain. Take shopping: When I felt bad, I'd run out and buy something. That happy feeling the purchase provided eventually faded. Feeling uncomfortable again, I'd run back to the store for relief. Maybe I would make another purchase, eat another cookie, drink another beer, or find another man. Whatever the temporary fix happened to be, I had to constantly replenish it because the relief was fleeting. My efforts to find comfort did not provide me with the real relief I needed. Eventually the person, place, or thing no longer works, and in many instances begins to cause problems of its own.

To be free of the buried thoughts and feelings, we need to look inside and face those thoughts and feelings we have been trying to avoid. This is a key to fixing your picker. We can cover up the pain, we can ignore it for a time, but it never goes away until we've allowed ourselves to face it. Only after we recognize and deal with what we find can we experience healing and a sense of inner peace.

MY FAMILY SECRET

When I finally dedicated myself to meditating, my own uncomfortable feelings came up. However, this time I was ready. I had made a commitment to myself to continue in the practice no matter what. But what happened next shocked me. After meditating for increasingly longer periods of time, working up to my goal of twenty minutes a day to start, I noticed that shortly after settling into my meditative state, I'd begin to cry. I cried slowly at first. But eventually, every time I sat down to meditate, a torrent of tears streamed down my face. I sobbed uncontrollably until I was gasping for breath.

What I soon learned was that part of the reason I was crying was that I was carrying a painful family secret. I was carrying around pain from childhood that I had been pushing down and trying not to accept. Now, as a grown woman, I was finally beginning to address it.

The feelings kept coming up over and over again. As I would sit down to meditate, I would want to cry. I felt a heavy sadness in my chest. The longer I sat, the more vulnerable and frightened I would feel. Slowly, and over time, the reason for the painful feeling surfaced. The feeling or thought (almost like a small voice) told me that I was not wanted. I became confused. What was the voice? Where was it coming from? Who didn't want me? But more importantly, was it true?

I continued to meditate. Great swells of pain rushed up. I would blubber as the voice told me, "Nobody wants you." I quickly began to feel that this meditation stuff was overrated. In fact, I began to doubt the benefits of meditation, thinking I'd felt much better while I was avoiding the pain I was now experiencing. This was way too much pain . . . and for what? I began to have misgivings. From where I was sitting, it seemed like a never-ending river of hurt that was flowing through me. I just wanted it to stop.

Day after day the voice would tell me, "Nobody wants you." But instead of diminishing over time, the voice became louder—"NOBODY WANTS YOU!" Then the voice got meaner, hissing, *"Nobody loves you."* My grief was so heavy; it felt like a lead weight was crushing my chest. The tears stung my eyes as every molecule in my body resonated with the words *nobody wants you, nobody loves you.*

I couldn't take this anymore. It was Christmastime and my mother was in town. I decided to tell her what was going on.

I said, "Mom, there's something bothering me." I then explained about my meditation practice and the voice I was hearing, then stated, "I have this feeling that when I was growing up, I was not exactly wanted."

I looked at my mother, both pleading for an answer and not wanting to know.

After a long pause, my mother sighed, "Yeah…that is probably true."

Whoa! I was in shock. One part of me said, "Yes, I knew it! I knew it! That makes sense." I was excited; I wasn't crazy. The voice was right. What a relief.

But the other part just wanted to die. Oh, my God, I really hadn't been wanted. My heart ached. A naïve part of me wanted to believe that all children are wanted. I wanted to believe parents always love their children. I thought, My God, who would ever love me if my own mother didn't?

The pain of my mother's admission was intense. I went from feeling strong and motivated to feeling as weighed down as if someone had just draped me with a coat of lead. But at the same time, things were finally beginning to make sense. The feeling of not being wanted had created an incongruence, or disconnect, in my life—and now I found out that I was *right* to feel that way, not crazy. I really hadn't been wanted. It was not my imagination. As my mother went on to explain herself, confusion between what I felt and what I thought I should feel began to dissolve. My mother's confession was painful, yet validating at the same time.

There had always been a small voice nagging at me, like a small child tugging on my shirt, demanding to be heard. I was finally able to give that voice the attention it wanted and so silence its incessant pestering. I felt a relief, but it would take more work to heal, find acceptance, and discover the devastating effects this had had on my life. With time, and more meditation, I would begin to understand my mother's words and the reasons behind them. Eventually, I would begin to empathize and forgive. You will read how later in this book.

It was through journaling that I realized the effect that this voice had had, and was still having, on me. Even though, without realizing it, I'd spent years trying to ignore it or run from it, deep down I had been listening to it. It was like background noise, a low, dull ache that I had been carrying around for years. This had to be a big piece of my broken picker, attracting me to relationships where I was not loved because that feeling was familiar. Now, in meditation, I was finally hearing it, finally releasing it. Every tear I shed released me from this pain and from the effects this pain had had on my life.

Please don't fear tears. They are healing. We are releasing all that pain and negative energy. We are freeing that space for happiness, light, and love. I look at this experience in the same way I look at getting a vaccination. When I was a child, I feared the shot because I didn't want to experience the pain. I couldn't understand why adults around me wanted me to hurt, and even said it was good for me. I understand now that the brief flicker of pain I experienced was minuscule compared to what would be the devastating effect of the disease that it was intended to prevent.

The tears experienced during meditation are tough for the moment, but minor compared to the long-term destruction caused by holding the pain inside. The release produces relief. That's one of the reasons I love tearjerker movies. Someone looking at me as I watch the film and cry might wonder why I would voluntarily view something that would make me cry. But I do. Many of us do. Why do we do it?

Because it makes us feel better. We release old emotions and walk out of the movie feeling lighter. The same is true with tears in meditation. We are cleaning out all that old stuff. Soon you will start feeling lighter because you are not weighed down by the past. It's like a good spring cleaning. It takes some work, but it's so worth it. You remove all the unnecessary clutter. You feel healthier and fresher, like when you crawl into a bed with clean sheets. An old Jewish proverb says, "What soap is for the body, tears are for the soul." Your tears have a cleansing effect on your soul and a healing effect on your picker.

BEGINNING MEDITATION

Fortunately, there are many ways to meditate, so there's sure to be one that's right for you. I found a chanting meditation easiest when I was beginning. But if you don't like to chant, you can simply sit and listen to the sound of the air moving through your nostrils as you breathe in and out. Whatever type of meditation you decide to try, be sure you are in a comfortable posture, wearing nonrestrictive clothing. Sit or kneel, or, if you are flexible enough, get into the famed "lotus position," with your legs crossed. If you meditate lying down, try not to become too comfortable or you may end up falling asleep, as meditation tends to be very relaxing after a while.

The chanting meditation I started with is called *japa* meditation; it involves the repetitive speaking of a *mantra,* that is, a sound or short phrase that helps you focus. The Sanskrit word *japa* is derived from the root *jap,* meaning "to utter in a low voice." A *mantra* is an energy-based sound that produces a specific physical vibration. The word *mantra* is derived from two Sanskrit words. The first is *manas,* or mind, and the second is *trai,* meaning to free from or liberate. Therefore, the word *mantra* means to free yourself from your mind. Think of it as freeing yourself from negative self-talk and freeing yourself from all the noise that blocks you from hearing your true self. Some say meditation is the art of listening to God, while others believe you listen to your own soul. Some say meditation can dissolve any sense of separateness or alienation. Most agree that it's a wholesome and harmless practice that can bring many benefits. So don't worry about doing it "right."

Why use a *mantra*? Love emanates from our heart and our soul, but the signals they send encounter interference, like static, from the noise in our minds. We must liberate ourselves from the noise in order to open up a passage for love to freely spring forth, without emotions such as fear and jealousy stemming from our minds. We release the negative energy of these emotions and become more grounded through meditation. The *mantra* is spoken repeatedly in order to clear the mind. That's the chanting part. The most common *mantra* is OM, pronounced "oh-mmmm." The OM meditation is considered the "root" *mantra*. It has also been called the primordial seed of the universe. It is believed by Buddhists that creation itself was set in motion from the sound of OM.

TO BEGIN

To do *japa* meditation, you begin by getting into a comfortable position. This could be cross-legged on the floor, sitting in a chair, or lying down. (The last is okay as long as you don't fall asleep; some experts caution against lying down to meditate.) Make sure your back is as straight as possible. If you are sitting cross-legged, you'll want your knees to be at the same level as your hips. If your hips are lower than your knees, sit on a firm cushion or perhaps a phone book to raise yourself up. The reason for having your knee and hip joints at the same level is to avoid stressing your knee joints.

Next, close your eyes. Be aware of your body—its temperature, its comfort level. Orient yourself physically, perhaps thinking, "I am in my room. I am sitting in a chair. My feet are on the floor"—whatever is applicable. The point of becoming aware of your physical body is to anchor yourself in the here and now. Take a deep breath through your nose, allowing your chest and belly to rise. As you exhale, say, "OOOHMMMM," the entire time you are exhaling. You will need to use your lips to form the "OH" sound, but as you begin the "MMMM," close your mouth and allow the vibration to resonate in your nasal chambers. Once the breath is completely exhaled, inhale again through your nose and repeat the exhalation. When you first begin practicing this, a few minutes' duration is great. Your goal is to eventually meditate for up to twenty minutes a day. If thoughts come into your head, don't resist them, but don't hold onto them either. In your mind, just say "hello," allow them to pass, and then refocus your attention on your breathing.

When you have completed the meditation, slowly open your eyes. Take a few deep breaths and reorient yourself with your environment. Look around the room, noticing your familiar surroundings. Take a minute to notice how your body feels. It's common after this meditation exercise to feel relaxed but energized.

Other types of meditation include dynamic meditations and creative visualization. Dynamic meditations are meditations in motion. The simplest of these is "walking meditation," in which you pay close attention to your movements and your breathing as you walk a path that is already familiar to you. Practices such as yoga (placing your body in certain postures) and *t'ai chi* (repeating a pattern of movements that look almost like a dance) are called dynamic meditations because they allow you to free yourself from your mind by focusing on your body and your breath. You shut off the noise in your head by focusing on a sequence of movements. The thoughts are diminished because your mind is absorbed in your movements and your breathing.

Creative visualization is usually done with the help of another person who guides you verbally as you imagine yourself in different settings. For example, the guide describes an imaginary journey for you to take, without leaving the room. Creative visualization can also be used to picture a situation you would like to be in. Creative visualization makes use of our inborn mental and physical capacities for imagining everything from taking our first steps as a tiny child, to putting together a creative project, to planning our lives. In fact, later we will use a form of creative visualization to help you picture your heart's desires. Once you know what you want, then you can use the techniques you are learning in order to manifest your wishes.

Meditation has been used for centuries to help release negative energy, achieve balance and groundedness, and find happiness. I encourage you to experiment and find out which of the various types of meditation works best for you. You don't have to worry about doing it right; the only wrong way to meditate is to not meditate. When the feelings come up, feel them and release them, but don't give up on your practice.

My tears removed the bitterness and hurt that made me hard. The flow of tears softened me as the flow of water in a river smoothes the rough edges of the rocks on the riverbed. My tears, no longer prompted by defensiveness, diminished, and as they left, they allowed me to be more open and loving. They washed away the protective cocoon I didn't know I was in, a protective shell that made a loving relationship impossible.

Persevere until you find the tears. Then rejoice as they fall, because you are well on your way to love.

Activity:

- ♥ Meditate every day with the goal of reaching at least twenty continuous minutes per day. Do this in increments, even if it means meditating only for a minute or two at first. Don't set an unrealistic goal for yourself. Meditation isn't like taking a pill and feeling its effect on you moments later; rather, it's a skill that you develop over time, through practice.

CHAPTER SEVEN

Step Four

Journaling: Gaining Self-Knowledge

"I WANT, BY UNDERSTANDING MYSELF,
TO UNDERSTAND OTHERS.
I WANT TO BE ALL THAT
I AM CAPABLE OF BECOMING."

—KATHERINE MANSFIELD

What is journaling? Quite simply, journaling is a way to grow in understanding of yourself and others in your life by writing down your thoughts and feelings as they happen over time. It is a powerful way to accelerate personal growth, reduce stress, and gain valuable self-knowledge, and it is an excellent tool for dealing with traumatic events in your life. It also helps us to gain critical information to repair and heal our picker.

Journaling is not to be confused with keeping a diary. A diary tends to be a laundry list of activities, whereas journaling is working with your thoughts and emotions about your life experiences. You can begin by writing down the events of the day, but the goal of journaling is not only to record what happened, but to reflect on how the events affected you emotionally.

A study published in the *Journal of Behavioral Medicine* took a look at patients' writings. The study showed that patients who expressed their emotions, particularly their anger, in their writing experienced a reduction in the severity of their anger and an improvement in their mood.[1] This observation gives us a hint of how powerful journaling can be, but there are many more benefits than the study referenced above reveals.

---

1 Graham, Jennifer, et al. "Effects of Written Anger Expression in Chronic Pain Patients: Making Meaning from Pain." *Journal of Behavioral Medicine* (June 2008), 31(3): 201–212.

BENEFITS OF JOURNALING

Journaling helps you to form thoughts and clarify them. Many times we have random thoughts and feelings that may seem to have no rhyme or reason, and yet they cloud our minds. Journaling allows us to filter these and find greater clarity. As we start jotting down what's going on inside us, what we're experiencing begins to either make more sense or simply stop bothering us. Some feelings we do need to sort through to get down to the root causes, while others we simply need to acknowledge and then let go of.

Beginning journaling is akin to turning on a light. Your feelings become more visible and the images become clearer. Women with broken pickers have usually spent their emotional lives in the dark, when all they needed to do was flip the light switch. (Face it, if we could have seen clearly, we would have run from many of the men we chose.)

In addition to clarifying your thoughts, journaling also allows you to test your thoughts before communicating them with other people. Many times, when we have a lot of emotion behind a thought we can overreact to small triggers. When we write about our thoughts and the emotions behind them, it forces us to take a pause, to think before we react, and to develop a response that will produce more positive results.

Journaling also can reduce the stress of past traumatic events. On March 11, 2004, during the peak of the morning rush hour in Madrid, a terrorist group attacked, detonating ten explosive devices on four commuter trains near the city center. One hundred ninety-one people were killed and 1,755 injured. Many thousands more were not physically affected but were mentally affected. Many suffered from stress-induced symptoms such as night terrors.

Researchers decided to study a group of survivors to find out if journal writing would benefit them. They randomly assigned participants to write down their thoughts and feelings about the attack. The study showed that the group that wrote expressed fewer negative emotions when asked to recall the trauma two months later than did the group that did not journal.[2]

Journaling has been found to be especially beneficial when dealing with negative emotions, particularly anger and resentment. The word *resentment* comes from the Latin word *sentire,* which means "feel." Therefore, "re-sentment" is literally the experience of "re-feeling" something. When we are angry with someone, we're feeling something negative. If the anger passes, as it often does, all is well. However, when we resent someone, we re-feel the anger as we think about it, which ends up producing stress, a bodily response that includes increased heart rate and blood pressure. Over time, this can have an injurious effect on our bodies. Journaling can help reduce the harmful effects of stress and provide a much-needed release from some of the obsessive, angry, or negative thoughts—the resentments—that people, especially women in poor relationships, may have. These tend to be the thoughts we re-experience as obsessive, self-defeating thinking.

Little girls are often taught to be sweet and nice. They are encouraged to display polite behavior. Emotions like anger and disapproval are particularly discouraged. Many times, because of this early training, our negative emotions get suppressed. This suppression can cause us to become disconnected from ourselves. We don't display or express the full depth and breadth of our authentic emotions. We can become afraid that if we show negative emotions we will be met with disapproval, rejected, punished, or criticized for exhibiting "improper behavior."

Over time, the suppressed emotions can fester. We discover glimpses of them when we overreact to everyday situations. Our actions and overreactions may be covering up an underlying resentment. These old suppressed emotions can even cause a barrier to intimacy without us

---

2   Itziar, Fernandez, and Paez, Dario. "The Benefits of Expressive Writing after the Madrid Terrorist Attack: Implications for Emotional Activities and Positive Affect." *British Journal of Health Psychology* (February 2008), 13 (pt. 1): 31–34.

realizing it. Developing a loving union with another human being can be very difficult while you are harboring feelings of anger and resentment, not necessarily for something that person has done recently, but for something that occurred long in the past. Those feelings can prevent you from having a fully open and loving heart and the healthy loving relationships you desire.

Journaling can unlock these suppressed emotions and free you to relate more directly and openly to the present moment. By continuing to journal, you can uncover and reach the ancient emotions that may be blocking you from the love you want. Journaling gives you a safe place to explore and release them.

REDUCING STRESS

When feelings of anger and resentment come up, our very natural and normal fight-or-flight response can be activated, producing a whole cascade of hormonal responses. Our nervous system prepares the body for physical activity—mainly, to fight or run. It increases alertness, heart rate, and blood glucose concentrations. This can cause you to be hyperalert, maybe wringing your hands and pacing the floor waiting for "his" call.

Stress hormones, like epinephrine and cortisol, suppress your immune system. Prolonged stress weakens the effectiveness of your immune system and increases your susceptibility to illness, such as infections and certain types of cancer. Prolonged stress can also produce depression.

When the fight-or-flight response is turned off, the "rest and digest" division of the nervous system kicks in. It has a calming effect on the body. Energy expenditure is reduced, digestion and waste elimination are restored, and normal bodily maintenance occurs. When you write down your feelings, you release them and the physical effects they have. You are then able to react to situations in a rational manner.

MY JOURNALING JOURNEY

As I continued to meditate and journal, I began reaching raw emotions. Waves of anger and sadness would surge forth. I was sad that my mother hadn't wanted me when I was young. I was angry with God. If God loved me, why would He have given me to a mother who didn't want me? If God really loved me, why would He let her take me away from my father, who did love me, to live with a man who was obviously annoyed by my existence? If God loved me, why did I have to go through all this pain and suffering? I realized through my journaling that I needed to come to grips with these questions.

Since I could not sit down with God and ask questions, I did the next best thing and sat down with my mother. With the help of a therapist I was able to discover the answers to questions that had plagued me my whole life. I came to accept and understand my mother's plight. At nineteen she was a divorced single parent, having run off with a man at age sixteen, not because she was in love with him but because she was fleeing an alcoholic home. I understand that she loved my father, but she had been ill-equipped for marriage and motherhood. Her fears and insecurities robbed her of any happiness, until eventually she left my father for another man.

I was coming to terms with all of this. I was happy that my mother was being honest with me. She could easily have lied, believing somehow that it would protect me from pain. But she was honest, and her honesty released me from my pain. Now that the truth was out, I was finally free to grieve. I developed empathy for her and could easily see myself making some of the same decisions. But more importantly, I was able to see how those early experiences and memories had affected my life.

I began to see how these past experiences affected my present relationships and the part they'd played in forming my picker. I was beginning to see how, when we don't trust ourselves, we become vulnerable to that which is untrustworthy in others. I was so busy trying to deny the truth that I was naturally matching up with men who couldn't be truthful. Reality was too painful; prior to this work I had preferred a nice illusion.

My underlying belief was that I was not lovable. As a result, I naturally was inclined to be attracted to men who couldn't love me. That was at the core of my broken picker. In fact, if I happened to find a man who loved me, I would either leave him for someone who was more in line with my underlying belief system, or I would do something to damage the relationship so he wouldn't love me anymore. Either way, I ended up reconfirming my belief that I was unlovable.

Now that I had discovered my self-sabotaging thought, I was free to deal with it. Through my journaling I had come to understand it, and through positive affirmations (which you'll read about in the next section) I was able to rewrite those negative thoughts—especially those beliefs about God and my value in the universe.

JOURNALING: HOW TO START

This may seem obvious, but to start journaling you need—a journal. There are many different types you can get, ranging from an expensive, leather-bound version to a simple, inexpensive spiral notebook. I prefer a spiral-bound-type journal because it allows me to fold it over on itself, making it more comfortable to write in while sitting up in bed. Choose whatever type you feel you will use. Avoid any that are so exquisite that you don't want to "ruin" them by actually writing in them.

Next, choose the time of day when you will journal. It is important to choose a time that allows you to be consistent. I've found that journaling works best if I write at about the same time every day. Daily journaling provides the maximum benefits.

Some people prefer to journal at night. I began journaling at night when my chaotic mind would not let me fall asleep. As soon as I placed my head on the pillow my mind would begin to race. It did not matter how tired I was; my swirling thoughts would not allow me to fall asleep. Or, even worse, I'd fall asleep only to be awakened by my racing mind in the middle of the night. It would take me several hours to fall back to sleep, and then I would wake the next day, tired and irritable. I learned that when I wrote in my journal at night, my thoughts were placed on paper and were no longer spiraling around in my head. I was free to sleep peacefully.

Some people prefer morning journaling. Journaling at night gets them agitated, rather than relaxed, or they find themselves too tired at night to journal. They find that journaling upon awakening in the morning allows them to jump-start their day and organize their thoughts.

Whatever time you choose, just make sure you can be consistent and not be hurried. Choose a time that allows you ample time to write. You will not fully experience the benefits if each time you sit down to write you are worried about all the other things you need to do.

WHAT TO WRITE IN YOUR JOURNAL

If you are like me, with lots of thoughts spiraling around in your head, the answer to what to write in your journal is easy. You begin by writing down those thoughts. Don't worry if your writing does not seem to make much sense. Don't worry about spelling or punctuation. No one will ever read it, maybe not even you. I have had journals that I looked at years later that made absolutely no sense to me. But the process of writing itself has had a powerful impact on me while I was doing it.

- Write about exactly how you feel about anything and everything, and feel free to pour your emotions out onto the page.

- Write about things that keep bothering you. Soon, journaling will help you to see patterns in your life…particularly relationship patterns.

- Write about painful past events. The *Journal of the American Medical Association* reported a study showing that writing about a stressful experience reduces physical symptoms.[3] Sometimes those past events can bring up anger. A safe way to deal with that anger is the letter-writing technique. In your journal, write a letter to whomever you are angry with. This works even if that person is no longer living. The letter allows you to safely release your resentment. After you have felt the anger and released it, you can start the healing process of forgiveness.

- Write down your dreams. Some people believe that our dreams are the gateway to the subconscious. The theory of dream analysis suggests that what you dream about is what your subconscious is struggling with. For example, it is believed that if you dream you are driving a car, it signifies your ambition. However, if you dream you are a passenger in a car, it indicates that you feel you are taking a passive role in your life. Of course, within each person, and from person to person, the dream symbols may vary, and must be considered in context. Dream analysis is believed accurate by some and nonsense by others. Whatever your belief, you may find, as I did, that it can be an insightful and interesting way to begin journaling for the day, especially when you just don't know where to start.

Your goal for journaling is to write at least two pages a day, or for a set amount of time, say, half an hour, consistently. You may find as I did that I wrote more when something was bothering me. In fact, it was more difficult for me to write when things were going well.

I need to mention an important factor when it comes to journaling. Journaling must be safe. You want to make sure you are free to write

---

3   Smyth, J. "Effects of Writing about Stressful Experiences on Symptom Reduction in Patients with Asthma or Rheumatoid Arthritis." *Journal of the American Medical Association* (1999), 291 (14): 1304–1309.

down your true feelings. It defeats the purpose if you are worried that someone might see your journal. You want to make sure that it is secure and you are free to write down exactly how you feel without worrying about hurting anyone else. Journaling is something you do just for you. If you need to hide your journal or put it under lock and key, please do so.

I have had occasions when I was traveling with a group of people and didn't feel very comfortable bringing my journal. On those occasions I would write my feelings on a loose piece of paper. Afterward, I would rip it up and throw it away. Possessing the piece of writing wasn't important, but writing about the feelings and releasing them was essential.

CONCLUSION

Your goal is to write at least two pages in your journal or to write for half an hour every day. Journaling will give you a broader and more accurate view of yourself and your life's journey. It will help you hash out past traumas and release the emotions involved. It will help you uncover relationship patterns and the events that influence them. You will better understand why you are attracted to the men who attract you. You will gain valuable self-knowledge and discover what healing work you need to do to make better choices in the future. The practice itself is the important part. Don't worry about doing it perfectly. . . there is no such thing as "perfect" when it comes to journaling. Just do it.

Activity:

- ♥ Write in your journal every day, beginning while you are on your personal retreat.

CHAPTER EIGHT

Step Five

Positive Affirmations

"ALL THAT WE ARE IS THE RESULT
OF WHAT WE HAVE THOUGHT.
THE MIND IS EVERYTHING.
WHAT WE THINK, WE BECOME."

—PRINCE GAUTAMA SIDDHARTHA, FOUNDER OF BUDDHISM

Who we are, what we do, and how we react all depend on our subconscious self-talk, that is, what we tell ourselves about ourselves—in other words, what we think. When our self-talk is negative, it's like a broken record that plays the same old track over and over. Until we change the record, we will respond in the same way, particularly when we are choosing men. The good news is that your subconscious responds very well to being revised and updated. As the French poet and novelist Anatole France wrote, "To accomplish great things we must not only act, but also dream; not only dream, but also believe." That's what positive affirmations are all about. Positive affirmations are about healing negative beliefs and embracing positive beliefs. Underneath every broken picker are negative beliefs. In this chapter, you will learn how to rewrite the self-talk script, a critical step toward the life of your dreams.

WHY WE NEED A REWRITE

We are sent messages as children. These messages come from many places. Some are hopeful and uplifting, such as children's stories wherein good prevails. We may get messages of encouragement from supportive teachers and coaches. And one of the greatest messages of caring and acceptance that we get happens when we make a mistake and our family and friends love us anyway.

However, negative messages are also a part of life. For example, maybe we make a mistake and someone we care about gets mad at us, and that hurts. A teacher may not be supportive and encouraging, and so we feel judged and unworthy. Sometimes good doesn't prevail. Any negative message can cause some lasting damage that we carry forward in our lives. Even the most well-intentioned parent can inadvertently send the wrong message, or we misinterpret what they are saying and take their meaning in a negative way. All of these negative and judgmental messages are part of the broken picker. Imagine that they are like smudges on a lens and that you can wipe them off and thus see much more clearly what the world offers and what your real choices are.

Once, while I was shopping, there was another woman in the store with two rambunctious children. They were running around the clothing racks, playing hide-and-seek. One boy, in his exuberance, came running through a rack of clothes, pulling several garments off the hangers. Shirts and skirts flew in every direction. The mother turned bright red with embarrassment and snatched the boy by the arm. She yelled, "How can you be so stupid?" Tears of humiliation and pain welled up in the boy's eyes as the mother ushered him out of the store.

The mother was not trying to tell the boy that he was unintelligent. What she meant was he was not behaving appropriately for these circumstances; his behavior embarrassed her and caused damage to the store. What she meant was this behavior was stupid. What he heard was "I think you are stupid." Not only did the boy feel judged, but judged very negatively in the eyes of a person he loved. A parent may inadvertently send the message that the child is flawed or unacceptable when all she was really trying to say was that his specific behavior, at that moment, was unacceptable.

Damage can also occur when parents attempt to control a child's behavior by withholding love or affection from them, or when they reward them only if they act in a certain way. A child may gain favor by being mother's little helper. This can send a message that we must be a "little helper" if we wish to be loved, that we are not lovable just as we are by being ourselves. The message gets translated into painful self-talk that we may carry around with us for the rest of our lives, unless we consciously and deliberately change it.

Children can develop feelings of being unloved and unworthy even in a perfect family. At times the most loving parents can feel overwhelmed and inadequate, and it comes out in negative messages to the child. We all carry around negative messages from our childhood. Unfortunately, these negative messages become part of our unconscious beliefs and thus part of our picker. In fact, some psychologists tell us that by the time we reach the age of fourteen, ninety-nine percent of us have a well-developed sense of inferiority. We may be reacting to present-day situations based on these beliefs without even knowing they are there.

Women are much more prone to absorb and replay negative messages and to hurt themselves than men are. This is not to say men have not absorbed negative messages about themselves, but biology dictates that their responses are more overt. Aided by the wonder hormone, testosterone, men channel their reactions to negative self-talk into action. Violent sports like football or boxing may absorb some of this energy. On the extreme end of the spectrum, violence toward domestic partners or random strangers may be the result. It can be argued that war is an outcome of men's tendency to resolve their inner pain in overt action. Women, on the other hand, tend to keep this pain inside, and process it by means of negative self-talk and feelings of unworthiness, helplessness, and self-pity. Positive affirmations can write over this negative self-talk.

Through our meditation and journaling, different messages and feelings will come up. We will become increasingly aware of our negative self-talk and how it affects what we experience and what we do.

There are many different areas in your life that positive affirmations can be used to improve. I have chosen affirmations for this section that will help improve self-esteem, self-worth, and spirituality. They help to heal your broken picker and thus help you attract more love, happiness, and abundance.

As you go through these affirmations, put them to the "mirror test." Stand in front of a mirror and say the positive affirmation out loud to your reflection. If you can say it, feel it, and mean it, then you are in good shape in that area. However, if you can't say it, if you avert your eyes while saying it, or find yourself thinking, "This is stupid," you'll know that those are the very affirmations you need the most. They're the ones you need to repeat.

You can use positive affirmations in your daily meditation, repeating a phrase as you exhale. You may want to write down the affirmation you're working on and place it in your wallet, looking at it several times during the day. When I started doing affirmations, I printed out several of them and hung them in various locations in my home. I placed one above my computer and another above my hallway mirror. I even had one taped to my front door that reminded me I only had today and to get out there and enjoy it.

Our first affirmation is:

I Can Do This

As you go along in this process, you will have moments of doubt. You will have moments when you feel you can't continue whatever it is you are doing at that moment. The process you are going through in learning affirmations requires work and faith. Know that it is natural to resist. This resistance emerges as doubts and fears. No matter: Repeat the affirmation and remind yourself . . . I can do this! I am strong and I want to get better.

This affirmation is particularly important if you are tempted to run to a man for comfort whenever you start feeling lonely or needy. Remind yourself that you are strong. Tell yourself that there is someone out there for you, and he's waiting for you to get better. Tell yourself that going through this difficult learning process will finally attract someone who is worthy of you.

I Am Worthy of Love

This was a big one for me. Since I didn't feel wanted growing up, I concluded that there must be something wrong with me. It seemed like everyone around me was getting ample amounts of love—everyone except me. I deduced that since I didn't feel love, I must not be worthy of love. The fault, I believed, was mine.

My mother's disclosure that I was not wanted had a great transformative power. I couldn't know it at the time, but it would change my life. Of course, I had always felt unwanted and unworthy of love. But no one would ever speak it. In fact, my mother would deny such an ugly fact. She didn't want to be "that kind of woman," a mother who did not want her child.

And yet she was, and I felt it, deeply. I made that feeling part of my self-talk. This is how my picker made use of those early experiences: By experiencing the feeling of not being wanted but not being conscious of the source of that feeling, I assumed it had to be true; it had to come from me. There must be something wrong with me. I must be innately unlovable. I carried that feeling around subconsciously all my life and it affected every relationship I had.

Love is energy. It's much like the energy that powers your house. In order for you to receive the energy into your house, it needs to be connected to the main supply. Once you are connected, you are able to receive all the energy you need (as long as you pay your bill). However, if someone severs that line, you will lose the flow of energy. My belief that I was not worthy was akin to severing the line. I was not able to receive love because I believed I was unlovable.

A person's emotional energy has to be available in order for him or her to give or receive love. You can't earn love or manipulate your way into getting love. A person immobilized with unresolved pain may be unable to give or receive love. Once I realized this, and began utilizing the *I am worthy of love* affirmation, I was free to jettison my previous misconception and fully embrace a new reality—that I am loving and lovable.

I Am Worthy

Feeling that I was worthy of love was a huge leap for me. I didn't start out that way when I began to heal my broken picker, but I progressed with the work I had committed to do for myself. I discovered that this feeling of unworthiness was pervasive, and touched almost every facet of my life. A lack of worthiness can manifest itself in many different ways. You may have a general feeling that you will never get what you really want. Sometimes it seems that everyone around you is so happy, you wonder, "Why not me?" And because of this you incorrectly come to the conclusion that somehow you are not worthy of the good stuff life has to offer. When you feel unworthy of love, you are naturally attracted to men who will not provide you with love.

Because I didn't feel worthy, I would settle for less. If I had a choice of something that was not quite right, but was cheaper than something that was perfect, I would take the lesser item.

If I bought something and it broke right away, instead of bringing it back to where I'd purchased it, I would accept it. I would say, "Oh well, just my luck." I wouldn't say, "Hey, I have just as much right as anyone else to have this work properly."

This feeling of unworthiness kept me from speaking up for myself in many situations, particularly with men. I would give up and give in before I tried, because I didn't believe I was worth "fighting for." In fact, it would take a lot to get me just to stand up for myself. As a result, I frequently played the role of the victim, unconsciously (and mistakenly) believing that only victims had the right to love, compassion, and support. By this flawed "reasoning," being a victim was what gave me the right to complain or speak up for myself.

Things Happen for a Reason and for My Highest Good

I had many negative beliefs regarding my position in the universe that adversely affected my picker. I needed to reinforce my faith in the universe, to change my picker by developing a belief that the universe was working in my favor. To be able to move forward, I had to come to believe that things happened for my ultimate good.

When I was going through tough times in my life, I never believed that anything good would come out of my suffering. In fact, I thought God was cruel to force me to go through whatever pain I was feeling. I would wonder what good could ever come from this.

I once had a crush on a man. I thought he was the greatest. But for some reason or another, we never seemed to be able to get together.

One day he asked me if I would be willing to help advance his career and introduce him to a woman he believed could help him in his endeavors. I jumped at the chance to be close to him and show how useful I could be in helping him reach his goals.

I was so excited about being able to help him. Unfortunately, I discovered that after I introduced him to the woman in question, they started dating. I was sick to my stomach and felt like a fool. I thought this was proof positive that God did not like me.

A few months later the man called me. I still had feelings for him, and my pulse raced when I heard his voice. As he spoke, I hoped to hear him say that he had made a mistake by pursuing the other woman. I was hoping he would say he had left her and was ready to date me. What he said instead was "I wanted to be the one to tell you—I am getting married."

I was crushed. I knew for sure life was unfair.

It was very difficult for me to believe that in a loving universe this could be happening to me. I concluded that the universe must not be a loving place, a message that only strengthened my broken picker.

About eighteen months after that phone call, the man called me again. This time he finally said the words I wanted to hear. "I would like to go out with you." However, instead of being overjoyed at that statement, I was horror-struck.

You see, he was still married.

I was disillusioned and sad. How could a man I thought was so wonderful do something I considered so terrible? But then a strange thing happened. As I practiced my journaling and affirmations, I began to see things differently. Eventually my grief was replaced with gratitude. I began to believe that maybe, just maybe, things do happen for a reason and for my highest good.

I thought of the words I had often heard in my program of recovery: "Rejection is God's protection." In this case, I saw that God, who loved me, had protected me from hurt by having the man I was interested in choose someone else before I became too attached to him. By the time that man came back to call on me, cheating on his wife to do so, I had developed enough self-esteem to realize I didn't want to engage in that kind of behavior—even with a guy who was "the greatest."

When I think of it that way, my feelings are quite different and much easier to bear.

You could not have told me that my struggles would eventually turn into a book. I would have never believed that the lessons I was learning would eventually help other women. And never would I have guessed that my experience was setting me up for a love that, at an earlier time, I could not have imagined.

I Am in Abundance
One of the most powerful affirmations I used was "I am in abundance." This was the affirmation I needed and used the most. Prior to this, my belief in scarcity had left me trapped. I could not give up on a relationship, no matter how bad it was, because I believed that if I left the one I had, I would never find another. I may have known the relationship wasn't right for me, but I feared that if I ended it, I would be alone, and maybe never find anyone ever again.

I stayed too long in a marriage because of this belief. I wasn't really happy, and when I would talk to my mother about it, she would say, "Well, you know you could do a lot worse." Though she didn't realize it at the time, my mother was reinforcing the broken part of my picker. I believed I could do worse, but I didn't believe I could do better. So I stayed…and stayed.

Everything in my life was permeated with my belief in a lack of abundance, not just a lack in my relationships. I would stay in jobs for fear I would not find another. I was afraid to take risks because I feared failing. I went without or I bought a lesser item and tried to make do for fear of not having enough money. What I needed to learn was that I was in abundance. I needed to know that I had what I needed, and that if I released something, or something was removed from my life, there would be something better to replace it.

My belief in scarcity was reflected in my spending. I eventually learned that money is an energy flow, and when I blocked the outflow by hoarding it, I also slowed the inflow. Once I announced to myself that I was in abundance, the abundance began to flow. I had to learn to be affirming and say, "Yes, I am in abundance," instead of saying, "No, I cannot afford that."

As long as I spend wisely on things that are good for me, I always have enough money. When I spend money on things that are good for me, for my soul or my body—nutritious food, a health club membership, or a massage, for example—I always have enough. In fact, I have more than enough.

One day, after I had learned the affirmation of abundance, I wanted to buy supplies for a creative project I was going to begin. When I said "yes," and I made the purchase, money miraculously appeared. A check I had forgotten I was due showed up. On other occasions I would sell a painting. Once I became open and allowed the energy to flow, I discovered that I was truly in abundance. People with money understand this concept. That is why you must allow an outflow. I had to believe the universe would provide, and when I did, I was in abundance.

I Only Attract Loving, Honest Individuals

Sometimes after we have been hurt in a relationship we develop negative beliefs about men. Those negative beliefs both spring from and reinforce a broken picker. Although it may have been only one bad experience, we sometimes find comfort in sweeping generalities. If we have been cheated on, it is tempting to believe that all men cheat. We don't want to be the only one ever hurt by a cheating boyfriend, so it is comforting to think that all men cheat or all men lie. This comes from a mistaken belief that if we depersonalize the experience, it will not hurt as much.

Unfortunately, these beliefs then become our reality, because we incorporate them into our Guy-Picking System (GPS). These underlying beliefs that men cannot be trusted cause us to find men who cheat or lie. When we believe that men cheat, we will naturally gravitate toward men who cheat. It's the basis behind the law of attraction; we attract what resonates in us most.

Have you ever met someone who believes the world sucks? They never seem to have a shortage of complaints. While you found the parking spot nearest the building, they had to walk three blocks…in the rain. The food they order in a restaurant is never right, and they crashed their hard drive and lost their work last week. Their beliefs are like magnets for troubles.

When it comes to love, any negative beliefs about men end up blocking us from the intimacy and trust we desire. Since these doctrines of distrust do not serve us, we must change them.

My Body Is Strong and Healthy

Positive affirmations can be used to heal your physical body. People have used positive affirmations for many types of healing. This has been well documented elsewhere. Maybe you are experiencing health problems, or maybe there is a part of you that you do not like. Maybe you wish you had smaller ears or fewer freckles. Maybe you feel you could be more outgoing if you had smaller thighs. For your life to get better—to heal—

it is important to accept yourself just the way you are, and work toward changing the things you believe need improvement. Positive affirmations can help you eliminate negative habits that prevent you from having the degree of health you deserve.

I Am Willing to Forgive

Positive affirmations are used to heal relationships and repair your picker. We can never be fully open to love and loving until we are at peace with ourselves and the universe. In order to be at peace with the universe, we need to be at peace with the people in it. To find this peace, we need to forgive. Forgiveness is not about letting someone off the hook for wrongs he or she has done. Forgiveness is about letting go of our attachment to the person or to the actions. Forgiveness is about us. When we forgive, we set ourselves free. When we forgive, the person who wronged us doesn't sleep better; we do. The person may not ever know you forgave him or her, but you will, and it will release you to love and be loved. Buddha taught that holding onto anger is like grasping a hot coal with the intent of throwing it at someone else; you are the one getting burned. To be a fully loving person, you must forgive.

I Am Beautiful, Inside and Out

Most of my life my feelings about myself fluctuated. It was like a roller coaster; one day I was up and the next day I was down. One day I was on top of the world and the next day I needed to look up to see the curb. Some days when I would dress up to go out and felt I looked really good, I had an air of conceit. I thought I looked beautiful, but not in a healthy, appreciative way. It was in an in-your-face and I-am-full-of-myself sort of way. I would build up a mask to cover up my feelings of inadequacy, like a little boy whistling in the dark. I didn't feel beautiful on the inside; my beauty at that moment was strictly visual. If I walked into a room and felt I was one of the most attractive women there, I would be comfortable. And I usually had a miserable evening. I was just not comfortable with myself, as myself, on a day-to-day basis. My insecurity created a social awkwardness (always an attractive quality!). I just couldn't figure out why I wasn't a man-magnet.

As I got older, I developed some level of comfort with myself. But now I was competing with a younger and younger crowd. It seemed as if I were chasing my tail. Until I was satisfied that I was perfect just as I was, I would always experience anxiety. By using this affirmation—*I am beautiful, inside and out*—I slowly began to believe that everyone was beautiful (including me) in their own way. I did not have to compete for attention because I knew I was beautiful inside. The more I developed a healthy self-confidence, the less I needed outside validation (the type of validation that usually led me to choose the wrong men). As I became more comfortable with myself, people became more comfortable with me. People became more attracted to me…and some of those people were emotionally healthy men who were also comfortable with themselves.

My Ultimate Purpose Is to Love and Be Loved
The final affirmation that I used reminded me of why I was doing all of this. Some days I would get frustrated and want to give up. My internal critic would tell me this was stupid and would not lead me anywhere. To counter this I would remind myself that my ultimate purpose was to love and be loved—this was the goal that I held for all affirmations. I was doing this work because I wanted to choose a healthy partner to love and to be loved by.

CREATING YOUR OWN AFFIRMATION
There are many positive affirmations that can be used to fix and heal your Guy-Picking System and begin making choices for a fuller, more loving, and more satisfying life. Hundreds of books have been written on positive affirmations and creative visualization. You may want to use some of those or create your own. The key to a successful affirmation is that it must be a positive, proactive statement, not a rejection or a negative statement. For example, you might say, "I have the power to

choose," instead of saying, "I am not a victim." By saying you are not a victim you are trying to convince yourself that you are not a victim, but the underlying message to your subconscious is that you are still a victim. Ironically, this type of affirmation reinforces the very belief you're trying to change.

Choose "I am" statements, such as "I am beautiful, powerful, and healthy." Statements such as "I don't want to be fat" or "I don't want to be lonely" only affirm what you don't want rather than what you do want. Statements such as "I am slim," or "I am becoming the perfect weight for me," or "I have many good friends who love and support me" move you toward your goal.

Similarly, statements such as "I hate my hair" or "I want a boyfriend" get you nowhere. When you declare you want something, do you know what you get? The wanting. You reinforce the desire and not the attainment and ultimate enjoyment of what you affirm. Start with what you truly want. Then develop affirmations stating that you are grateful that you have already acquired that which you desire. Proclaim that you already possess what you want. In fact, some of the most powerful affirmations are announcements of gratitude for having what you want, such as "Thank you, God, for my good health."

CONCLUSION

Positive affirmations are powerful tools for creating the life you want. Use them to rewrite any negative beliefs that are part of your broken picker or to strengthen positive beliefs you are developing. Use them to heal your relationships and your body. Positive affirmations can be created to improve any aspect of your world, because they are giving you new ways to see the choices that are available to you, beyond any of the present limitations of your picker.

Repeated affirmations, over time, will make themselves felt in your thoughts and your behavior. As you continue using positive affirmations, you will feel your broken picker begin to heal. And once that happens, you'll start to see amazing changes in your life, especially your love life, as you start to attract the love you desire.

Activity:

- ♥ Repeat at least two or three affirmations every day.
- ♥ Write them down on a sticky note, index card, or piece of paper and place them where you will see them frequently.
- ♥ Place a small card containing your most important affirmations in your wallet or above your mirror.

CHAPTER NINE

Step Six

Pamper Yourself:
Loving Yourself

"SELF-LOVE, MY LIEGE, IS NOT SO VILE A SIN
AS SELF-NEGLECTING."

—WILLIAM SHAKESPEARE

*Y*ou have been working hard. You have been on a personal retreat; you are journaling, meditating, exercising, and eating right. You deserve a reward—right? Well, guess what? Now you get one. This section is all about indulgences. You are going to reward and nurture yourself by pampering yourself.

WHY?

Instead of asking, "Why pamper myself?" ask, "Why not?" Why wouldn't you want to pamper yourself? You are sending a message to the universe about how you want to be treated. This will help create a new underlying belief system within yourself that will have a positive effect on your picking system. No one will treat you better than you treat yourself. If you are gentle and caring with yourself, the world will become more gentle and caring. If, on the other hand, you are tough on and stingy with yourself, you will find that the world will confirm that also.

It is impossible to act in a manner that is inconsistent with the way we see ourselves. If you believe you are not worth spending money on, you will find a million reasons why you can't spend money on yourself. However, if you start pampering yourself and you are still held back by the core belief of your picker that you are not worth it, your efforts to pamper yourself will feel very uncomfortable. Your mind will come up with hundreds of reasons why you should stop, reasons that have to do with such things as money, time, and inconvenience. If you don't feel you are worth it, you will find other things that you "should" be doing, such as laundry, organizing your sock drawer, or finishing that afghan you started crocheting in the seventh grade…anything—except treating yourself well.

So why do we do this? Why do we say "no" to pampering ourselves? Maybe the same negative self-talk that fuels our broken picker tells us we aren't worth it. Well, if you continue to believe you are not worth being treated well, then it will be very difficult to begin to treat yourself well. And if you don't begin to treat yourself well, others will not treat you well, either. And so the cycle will continue. Keep in mind that your internal belief system—your picker—is being changed. As the change begins, you may very well encounter resistance. Your job is to feel the resistance but continue on course through it. You will need to stay consistently positive and affirming if you want the underlying beliefs of your picker to change.

By being good to yourself, you enhance your self-concept and self-esteem. You fortify the core of your personality and create a positive self-image.

LOVING YOURSELF HELPS COUNTER SADNESS

This is important. Through your journaling and meditation, sad feelings may be coming up. You may even find yourself grieving. Soothing yourself with self-nurturing activities helps you honor your feelings and keep on doing this sometimes difficult work. It's okay to feel sad; it just means you need to grieve. The reason you are grieving now may be that you would not allow yourself to grieve earlier. Perhaps at the time you suffered a great loss there wasn't the support system in place to allow you to grieve, or you were told that it was not appropriate to grieve, or you felt you had to show that you were invulnerable.

Feelings of grief are uncomfortable, so we tend to want to avoid them. You are not going to keep avoiding them. You are going to feel them, honor them, and release them. And as you do that, you are going to love and take care of yourself.

HOW?

Every week you will do at least one type of pampering activity. It can be as simple or as extravagant as you want. You may limit yourself because of finances; after all, we are worth spending money on, but we also want to be responsible to ourselves and our bank accounts. Sometimes, not spending money can be a way of treating yourself well, particularly if your past spending caused increased financial pressures and in turn made you feel unworthy. In some cases, cutting costs may be a way of treating yourself better. Remember, you are sending a message to the universe about how you would like to be treated. It is about treating yourself well and doing little things that make you feel good. So find a balance between financial responsibility and splurging on some self-nurturance. Some of the things you may want to do are:

Manicure/Pedicure

Few things feel as indulgent as a pedicure. Having someone massage and fuss over your feet provides an unparalleled luxury. It is wonderful to have your feet soaking in a warm, soothing foot bath, followed by a treatment that leaves your feet feeling and looking beautiful. Afterward, have your hands massaged and your nails done. It feels good to have stunning-looking nails and toes. You walk out of the salon like you are floating on air.

If you don't go to a shop to get it done, even painting your own nails at home gives you a renewed sense of beauty and confidence. You don't even have to show off your nails. The thought of having pretty nails inside your shoes can cause you to have a spring in your step.

Have Your Hair Done

Having someone else wash your hair and massage your scalp can feel heavenly. Getting a wash and style can add radiance. Why not try something different? Go in and have some fun. Get a new cut, or even spruce up your color. Try some highlights or maybe some lowlights. How about a completely different color? Look through magazines or ask female friends for suggestions. Try the style or color you have been secretly thinking about but have been afraid to try. The chemicals used nowadays are so gentle that if you don't like the color, you can always make changes. Go a little crazy, experiment, maybe even try extensions.

If having your hair done in a salon is not your thing, you can give yourself a salon treatment at home with a hot oil product to revitalize the luster. The important thing is to do something beautiful for you.

Whiten Your Teeth

This is an easy way to enhance your look and increase self-confidence. You can have it done in the dentist's office or you can do it at home. There are several different products on the market to choose from. When we feel better about our smiles we smile more, and wearing a smile is the easiest way to improve your looks.

Clean out Your Closet

This is a great way to feel unburdened. By removing old, worn-out items, you are freeing up space and letting go of the past. This symbolizes your desire to get rid of the old and make room for the new. The best part is that it costs you nothing, and you can even make money by donating the old clothes and taking the tax deduction, or reselling them at a consignment store or over the Internet.

Get a Massage

There are several theories about the benefits of massage. Besides the obvious one that it just feels good, massage has several bonuses. One theory states that your body holds tension in different areas. For example, when you have tension, your shoulders may stiffen up. Massage therapists call these stiffened areas "buttons." They produce "knots" in your muscles that can be massaged out. The theory is that once you massage out the knots, the tension these knots hold is released. Many people will tell how, the day after a massage, they felt sad or sometimes even angry. This is a very good thing; it means you are releasing the energy of that stored emotion. Proponents of massage believe that we can carry around pain for years, trapped in our bodies. Massage can help release it.

The great news is that not only does massage help release emotional pain; massage can also soothe physical pain. You may be familiar with this mechanism that you unconsciously employ when you bang your elbow. The pain is eased by rubbing the area. This occurs because of stimulation of pressure sensors in the skin that release chemicals that inhibit pain. The rubbing of the area helps to decrease the sensitivity of the area and any pain is eased. So massage also has pain-relieving benefits.

The Spa Treatment

If your finances permit, visit a spa for a day of beauty. There are several different types of spa treatments to choose from. You may begin with a massage, then a sauna, and then a facial. A facial consists of deep cleaning of the skin, exfoliation of the top layer of dead cells, and extraction of blackheads. An esthetician will then give you a facial massage to relax and stimulate your skin and muscles. Finally, you will receive a mask to help treat and tone your face. It is a wonderful experience that leaves you feeling refreshed and looking younger.

You don't have to go to a spa to get the spa treatment. You can give yourself a luxurious experience right at home. Draw yourself a hot bubble bath. Throw in some aromatic bath beads or soothing bath salts. Turn off all the lights and light some candles. Put on calming music or a recording of some positive affirmations. Apply a facial mask and allow the experience to wash away any negativity you may be feeling.

I once lived in a place that didn't have a bathtub, just a shower. But I used to love to light a few candles and close the bathroom door. The room had no windows, so it was lit only by the faint glow of the candles. I would put on a CD of rain forest sounds while I took a long, hot, sumptuous shower. Any problems that I had would wash away with the soap bubbles.

Candles, Aromatherapy, and Essential Oils

Scented candles, bath beads, and essential oils are all part of aromatherapy. Aromatherapy works by stimulating the smell receptors in your hypothalamus. The hypothalamus is involved in a variety of emotional responses, including anger, aggression, fear, pleasure, and contentment. Therefore, certain smells can evoke an emotional response. For example, the smell of cinnamon is associated with coming home to a place of safety and comfort. That's why some people recommend placing cinnamon in a house that is for sale when potential buyers are due; it is theorized that the cinnamon smell will make prospective homeowners feel that the place is already "home."

The hypothalamus also lies along the memory pathway. That is why certain smells can evoke strong memories. For example, the smell of apple pie may cause you to remember a visit to your grandmother's house or to a wonderful bakery where you found comfort foods such as cinnamon rolls.

Different scents can evoke both positive and negative responses. Researchers have found that certain scents tend to evoke similar responses in most people. These scents are used frequently in aromatherapy and can be found in an easily usable form called "essential oils."

Essential oils are aromatic liquid substances that are extracted from different species of flowers, seeds, barks, leaves, roots, and trees. Essential oils have been used for years in medicines, cosmetics, and massage oils. They are used to treat many ailments, including digestive problems, headaches, and respiratory problems. The essential oil of eucalyptus is the active ingredient in many vaporizing chest rubs. The strong smell of eucalyptus helps open up nasal passages and can alleviate sinus headaches.

I use lavender oil a great deal. Lavender oil is the essential oil of healing. I use a diffuser, which is a container of water into which I place a few drops of oil. This is then held over a candle. The votive candle gently warms the water, filling the room with the warm, soothing scent of lavender. I have found this to be very comforting while I am writing or meditating. Rosemary is also a great oil to use while writing during the day because it has a stimulating effect. It is also sometimes added to baths to soothe sore muscles.

There are several essential oils used for general well-being. Jasmine is used to treat anxiety and depression because it has a wonderfully intoxicating scent and is soothing and sensual. It is also reputed to possess aphrodisiacal properties, promoting love and peace. Jasmine is also reported to help build confidence.

Ylang ylang is an essential oil that has a deep, rich scent with a hint of jasmine. Like jasmine, ylang ylang has aphrodisiacal properties and is used to decrease depression and promote a sense of well-being. Ylang ylang can be used at bedtime because it has a sedative property.

Bergamot is another essential oil used to treat depression, with a sweet, spicy scent. It's what gives Earl Grey tea its special flavor. It has a refreshing, uplifting quality that is best used during the day. It can be combined with other essential oils such as lavender or chamomile.

Basil is an uplifting essential oil that can be used to combat depression. Basil is best used during the day.

The effects of the essential oils have been documented over the centuries. Since our response to scents may vary, it is important to pick scents that have the desired effect on you. There are hundreds of different types of essential oils, but only about seventy are used in aromatherapy. These oils can be combined or used separately. Experiment and look for a scent that resonates with you. Find a store that has them and start sniffing.

Teas

Sipping different teas can be wonderfully self-nurturing. There are many unique combinations of herbs, leaves, fruits, flowers, and nuts. The aroma and warmth of the liquid is marvelously calming. After a long day, it can be relaxing to sit down with a warm cup of comforting tea. Some teas can uplift and stimulate, such as green tea. Chamomile teas have a wonderfully soothing and sedative effect. A cup of tea prior to bedtime can help provide a restful sleep. Just don't pick a tea with caffeine. Ginger and lavender teas have been used for de-stressing. Peppermint teas have been used for years to settle stomachs and reduce anxiety. Also, rose hip teas are reported to have an antidepressant effect.

Some herb teas and their common uses are:

Teas	Common Uses
Black cohosh	Treats menopause and PMS
Caraway	Treats digestive problems and anxiety
Cinnamon	Antispasmodic
Cloves	Painkiller
Echinacea	Stimulates immune system
Elderberry	Treats cold and flu
Eucalyptus leaves	Treats cough and cold
Fennel	Treats gas and colic
Ginger	Treats nausea
Goldenseal	Antibiotic
Hibiscus	Reduces cholesterol
Lemon balm	Mild sedative
Lemongrass	Treats indigestion and is a muscle relaxant
Marjoram	Antibiotic
Nettle	Strengthens and supports the whole body
Nutmeg	Digestion and skin ailments
Orange flower	Mild stimulant
Parsley	Treats blood disorders
Passion flower	Treats insomnia and headaches
Peppermint	Reduces anxiety
Rooibos	Antioxidant
Rose hips	Treats diarrhea
Rosemary	Stimulant
Sage	Treats gingivitis
St. John's wort	Treats depression
Saw palmetto	Treats genitourinary problems

Take a trip to your local tea shop or a natural foods store that carries a wide selection of teas. Taste different teas and experiment. Buy some honey if you like it sweet, and brew yourself a tasty cup of tea. Get yourself a fancy teaspoon, perhaps a lovely teapot, and taste, enjoy, and play.

Buy Yourself Some Flowers

If someone brought you flowers, would you feel good? Or course you would, but we sometimes scoff at the thought of buying ourselves flowers. Our internal critic says, "You don't need flowers, they are a waste," or "This is silly; they are going to just die anyway." However, if we bring flowers home and place them on a table, they make us smile. That is what self-nurturing is all about, that smile from your soul. So think of what can you do for yourself today to make you smile. Think about maybe buying yourself flowers.

Take Yourself out on a Date

Check out that new restaurant you heard about. You can explore alone (maybe take a favorite book or luxury magazine) or get a few girlfriends together to go with you. Have a girls' night out. With a couple of friends you can even indulge in that piece of chocolate cake. It is not as fattening when served with four spoons.

How about a day date? Get out into the sunlight today. Your body naturally produces serotonin during the day when exposed to the sun. Serotonin has a mood-elevating effect. Antidepressant drugs such as Prozac are called selective serotonin reuptake inhibitors (SSRI) because they work by blocking your body's reabsorption of serotonin, thereby allowing the mood-elevating effect to work longer. The sun exposure triggers your body to produce serotonin, so getting out into the sunlight has a mood-elevating effect. Exposure to light brighter than ordinary indoor light helps trigger serotonin. Taking a walk during the day, or having your lunch while sitting in the park or at an outdoor café can elevate your mood and decrease your chances of feeling depressed.

CONCLUSION

There are many wonderful ways to indulge and pamper yourself (I bet you can think of others on your own). Pampering sends a message to the universe about how we want to be treated and changes the type of man we are attracted to. Pampering soothes and supports us, making us feel loved. It helps decrease pain, helps us work through pain by allowing us to grieve, and elevates our mood. So get out there and spoil yourself.

(I knew you would like this chapter.)

Activity:

♥ Treat yourself to at least one pampering activity each week.

CHAPTER TEN

Step Seven

Do Something New: Changing Your Beliefs

"YOU MUST DO THE THINGS
YOU THINK YOU CANNOT DO."

—ELEANOR ROOSEVELT

*T*his section is about changing beliefs. If you want to change the men you are picking, you need to start with the underlying beliefs about yourself and your abilities. The way to change your beliefs is through action. You are going to walk through your fears and *act* your way into a new way of thinking. The actions you will be taking might be something new, perhaps something you think you cannot do. As you begin doing the things you think you cannot do, the things you have been telling yourself you cannot do, you will start by making small changes to your actions. The belief that you cannot do certain things will begin to collapse soon after you begin to prove to yourself that you really can "do the things you cannot do."

If your goal is to be in a loving, honest relationship, you must have virtues. To develop virtues we must act virtuously. Courage is an especially valuable virtue because it is what we need to try new things, to change, and to cope with difficult emotions and difficult situations. It's the root word of "encourage"—to promote, raise hopes, take interest, and give sympathetic advice.

How do we act courageously? By facing our fears and trying something new. Mark Twain once said, "Do the thing you fear most, and death of fear is certain." With each fear that dies, we grow that much more courageous. When we become more courageous, we are preparing ourselves for love. Think about it: In order to love, you must be vulnerable. You can't truly love when you are guarded; you must open your heart to the other person. If we are fearful and guarded, we will naturally attract men who are guarded. If you want real love you must be vulnerable, which by definition involves risk. You can avoid risk entirely and keep your heart safe by never venturing out of your comfort zone to make yourself vulnerable in a relationship. You will be perfectly safe and invulnerable, but is that the way you want to live? If it were, would you be reading this book?

Having the courage to do something new can start us on the path of facing our fears. Through courage, we build confidence in ourselves. By repeatedly facing fears and building confidence—which we can only do through drawing upon our own reserves of courage—we feel safer and can be more vulnerable and open to love.

Before beginning this journey of personal change, my sense of being worthy was often manifested as defeatism. I would give up almost before I even started because my core belief was that I was not good enough anyway, so why bother? I would start many projects with great hope and optimism, but would quickly lose steam. I was afraid I was going to fail. Even worse, I was so sure I was going to fail that I gave up before starting, thus sparing myself the pain of failure. My belief that I was unworthy reinforced my belief that I would fail, undermining whatever courage I might have had.

The first time I completed a task thoroughly, from start to finish, I felt a sense of accomplishment—a sense of healthy pride. I also developed a memory to draw on, so that the next time I faced a new task, I could remember how it felt to be afraid and yet muster the courage to "do it anyway." As John Quincy Adams, the sixth president of the United States, famously said, "Courage and perseverance have a magical talisman, before which difficulties disappear and obstacles vanish into air." Act from courage, do what needs to be done, and see your obstacles begin to vanish.

Over and over again in our lives, we are presented with opportunities to face our fears and "do it anyway." Each time we do this, whether we succeed or fail in actually getting over our fears, we become more familiar with our courage and thus expand this virtue.

Our goal is to have a life full of love. Love takes courage. When we first find love, it can feel so wonderful that we fear it may end. We may hold on too tight, sabotaging it by strangling it, for fearing of losing it. We forget that healthy love is a free exchange. To allow for open, free exchange, you must overcome your fear of losing the love—this takes courage. By doing new things, we develop courage when the risk is low and the potential loss is minimal. As your courage expands, so does your ability to love freely and choose healthier men who can love freely also.

POTENTIAL AND GROWTH

Potential can be defined as the capacity for being, which is not yet in existence—something possessing the capacity for growth or development. You have potential. You have the ability to grow and develop, to be more tomorrow than you are today. And yet we often, almost deliberately, refuse to develop our potential. This is especially true for those of us whose pickers are broken. Psychologist William James wrote, "Most people live, whether physically, intellectually, or morally, in a very restricted circle of their potential being. They make very small use of their possible consciousness and of their soul's resources in general, much like a man who, out of his whole bodily organism, should get into a habit of using and moving only his little finger." One goal of this book is to help you develop your full potential for love and happiness.

You cannot love or be happy if you hold yourself back; you must have courage and grow. If you want a happy, healthy, and exciting partner, you must be happy, healthy, and exciting. By doing something new you expand your world and the types of men you have to choose from.

Most of us are familiar with goldfish. In fact, many of us had goldfish as children. We would keep them in little bowls of water with colored rocks on the bottom. The unique thing about a goldfish—a domesticated member of the carp family of fishes—is that it grows in proportion to the container it is kept in. When kept in a small bowl, goldfish stay small, growing to about an inch in length. If released into a large pond, they can grow up to twenty-three inches long and weigh more than nine pounds.

Our own human "goldfish bowls" are not necessarily physical. We have the physical, mental, emotional, and spiritual limitations we have imposed on ourselves—the foundations of our broken picker. If we have the courage to release ourselves from these restrictions—to consciously choose bigger bowls to live in—we can grow to our own full potential, physically, mentally, emotionally, and spiritually. When we expose ourselves to more and more opportunities, our growth potential and choices become virtually unlimited.

FIND YOURSELF

This may sound like a cliché—"I need to find myself"—but there is truth in every cliché. There is truth and there is irony, because in order to find yourself you must lose yourself. Think of your favorite actor. Remember a movie he or she was in that you enjoyed. Why was the performance great? Was it because he or she was nervous and self-conscious? No, of course not. The performance was great because the actor was immersed in the character. The actor was in the present moment, not thinking about what he or she looked like or what he or she would be doing next week.

When you are fully present and focused on the moment, you become fully yourself. The great Irish poet William Butler Yeats talked about the moment when a person becomes most fully him- or herself, and when that happens, "How can we tell the dancer from the dance?" We forget our inhibitions, even forget things like how unworthy we think we are or whether or not we're "doing it right," and we are just in the action itself.

When you become absorbed in an activity, you forget about yourself. In forgetting about yourself, your true identity emerges. You are focused in the here and now; you are fully present, with no past, no future, just now. It is in the now that your true self exists. When you discover your true self, it becomes much harder to buy into unhealthy illusions. You see yourself and the men you pick more clearly, becoming less likely to overlook or rationalize obvious character flaws.

Spirituality and creativity are parallel paths. Spirituality leads to greater creativity and creativity leads to greater spirituality. Creativity fosters a lifeline to God. By becoming immersed in a new activity, not only do we find ourselves, we also find God. We find new courage and transcend limitations we would otherwise impose upon ourselves. While learning and creating, we momentarily lose our self-centeredness, which allows our higher self to emerge. The greater our courage, the more we are able to get out of our own way, learn something new about ourselves, and discover that, regardless of our fears, we can do it…we can change our lives and our relationships for the better.

WHAT IF I FAIL?

Many of us say, "I would love to do that, but…". Then we give a laundry list of excuses why we cannot do a specific thing: "I am too old," "I am too young," "I am all thumbs," "I have two left feet," or "I can't afford that." I believe the American scientist George Washington Carver had it right when he said, "Ninety-nine percent of the failures come from people who have the habit of making excuses."

Often, we will not try something new because we feel inadequate to the task. Our fears hinder us. These fears prevent us from full involvement with the experiences we are given to help us grow. When we decide not to try something because of fear, we withdraw from life. We fear we might fail. When we do that, we have chosen instead a different type of failure—failure to be all we can be. Every experience can move us forward in the understanding of ourselves. When we choose not to participate, we stay stuck in a world we need to leave behind.

It might seem that changing these patterns would take a major overhaul. After all, patterns and mind-sets usually don't change radically overnight; they do, however, respond very well to small, incremental changes. By making little improvements, you can slowly change your old belief system, one flaw at a time. The key is to do it, to tackle those old myths and dispel them. That's exactly how you change your Guy-Picking System. We are going to reject our preconceived concepts of ourselves (our old myths) and inject a new and improved version. The first concept we are going to reject is "I can't do this."

No one would ever expect a child born prematurely in 1940 to survive, let alone to grow up to do great things. No one would expect a girl who spent her childhood in bed with scarlet fever and polio, losing the use of her left leg, to ever walk again. No one would ever expect that "handicapped" child to be athletic. But instead, the world stood in amazement as we watched Wilma Rudolph become "the fastest woman in the world" and the first American woman to win three gold medals in one Olympiad. She refused to use "I can't." You can, too.

From this day forward we will consider "can't" another four-letter word and remove it from our vocabularies. An acceptable substitute is "I will."

An important part of releasing old myths is just to do something new. Many times we refuse to tackle a new task because we are afraid we are not going to do it perfectly. Well, guess what? You're probably *not* going to do it perfectly the first time you try anything.

Thomas Edison frequently admitted that he had many more failures than successes. He experimented on more than six thousand different filaments before he found one that would work in his incandescent light bulb. If he had given up on the first couple of tries, the world would have been illuminated by flickering candlelight or smoky lanterns for many years longer that it was.

"Doing it perfectly," or even doing it well, is not the goal; simply *doing it is*—whatever you decide "it" is. Doing it and failing is fine. Not doing it is what's unacceptable. If at first you don't succeed, pick yourself up, dust yourself off, and do it again, learning from whatever mistakes you've made along the way.

Sometimes adversity can be a powerful motivator—that one key puzzle piece to make you successful. Theodore Roosevelt, our twenty-sixth president, was frequently stricken with severe asthma as a child. In an effort to improve Theodore's health, his father emphasized the need for Theodore to "make himself" physically, as there were few effective pharmaceutical remedies for asthma in those days—the disease was often deadly. Theodore took his father's philosophy to heart and became an enthusiastic proponent of "the active life." He'd work out for hours on gym equipment and became an avid outdoorsman. Although he never became a super-athlete, the former sickly child had developed excellent stamina by the time he entered college. In later years he rose to be, first, the governor of New York, and later, the only president to receive awards for his writing, the Nobel Peace Prize, and the Congressional Medal of Honor. During the Spanish-American War, he became famous as the irrepressible colonel of the "Rough Riders," a singular cavalry unit. Not bad for a sickly child who wasn't expected to see his fourth birthday. Without his physical difficulties to spur him on, Theodore Roosevelt might have been just another pampered rich boy, and our country might not have its magnificent system of national parks, which he, as president, initiated.

Being able to fail gracefully is important. Humility is born of being able to laugh at yourself. Children aren't afraid to try and fail repeatedly, but unlike grownups, they call it "having fun." Our goal is to have fun. Our goal is to be childlike and try something new.

If you believe you have two left feet and you cannot dance, take a dance lesson. In fact, take several dance lessons until you feel comfortable on the dance floor. It is okay that you probably will not make an appearance on *Dancing with the Stars*, but you never know. More amazing things than that have happened. I was once told by my teacher that I was a terrible writer. I had two choices: I could believe what he said and allow it to become part of me, or I could work on improving and reject his opinion. (I will let you decide which choice I made.)

EXPANDING YOUR GOLDFISH BOWL

What is your goldfish bowl? Do you believe you are bad with money? Join an investment group or a workshop on managing money. Do you believe you can't hold a tune or are tone deaf? Take a singing lesson or pick up an instrument. There was a time when I knew that I could not sing. My voice was deep, with little range, making it difficult to find songs I could manage. However, I decided to take singing lessons anyway. I worked with a wonderful woman who found some pieces of music that I could sing to. Not only did I take the lessons and learn to sing, I decided at the end to try out for a musical at the local theater. I was actually selected for the part of the cosmetics company president in a production of *Victor/Victoria* and had a wonderful time. The audiences seemed to enjoy it as well, but the most important thing was that I had destroyed the "power" that my fear of singing in public had had over me.

Are you shy? Do you fear getting up in front of people and speaking? Take a public speaking class or join an organization like Toastmasters. Some of the best speakers there have had the same fear. In fact, these organizations were started to help people overcome their fear of public speaking. Since people there have felt the same way you do, they will support you until you feel comfortable.

Do you believe you are not mechanically inclined? Take a shop class or a course in basic automotive repair. Believe you can't cook? Buy yourself a cookbook, and experiment. Turn on a TV cooking show and have fun. Maybe you don't want to cook because you already feel overweight. Then join a gym or start exercising at home on your own. Just a short walk in the evening can do wonders. Ask a friend to be your walking buddy. If she can't be there physically, have her call you to encourage you. Remember, big changes start with small improvements.

Is there something you would like to do but fear it is too late? Anna Mary Robertson Moses, better known as "Grandma Moses," was a renowned American folk artist. She did not start painting until she was in her seventies. She was almost eighty before she sold her first painting. She would eventually paint nearly sixteen hundred paintings before her death at age 101.

Your task is to find something new to try. It doesn't have to be a lifelong, nagging desire. Maybe it is something you have seen people do and were curious about, such as riding a motorcycle or even a unicycle. You could write a poem or grow vegetables in your backyard or on your deck. You could learn to knit, take a belly dancing class, or simply get a library card. Whatever it is—now is the time to do it.

A friend once told me he knew a woman who celebrates every birthday by doing something she fears—last year, it was parachuting from an airplane. Another time it was swimming with dolphins. We each have fears; why not do what this woman does? You may not get over them, but you'll have some great stories to tell.

The goal of this activity is to expand your comfort zone by getting past some of your self-limiting fears. Those are fears that have prevented you from being all that you can be, fears that can produce a broken picker. They are different from normal, healthy fears, such as the fear of jumping out of an airplane without a parachute or the fear of fire. Some fears are good to have and should be respected. The fears you want to overcome are the ones that have contributed to your broken picker and that are keeping you in your box. If you do something a particular way because that's the way it is done in your family, but secretly you would like to do it differently, then face that fear that's holding you back. If everyone in your family has always voted a straight party ticket, but you really want to vote for a different candidate this year, then do it.

In a healthy, loving relationship, both people must feel free to grow and change and still be loved; often this requires the courage you will have developed by facing your fears and growing. By rewriting the script of what's possible in your life, you will make better relationship choices and decrease the chance of sabotaging the love you will find.

Activity:

- ♥ Sign up for a new activity by the end of this week. Then pursue at least one new interest each month.

CHAPTER ELEVEN

Step Eight

Doing Something Good for Someone Else: Joy

"DOING GOOD TO OTHERS IS NOT A DUTY,
IT IS A JOY, FOR IT INCREASES OUR OWN
HEALTH AND HAPPINESS."

—ZOROASTER, PERSIAN PROPHET AND RELIGIOUS LEADER

*I*f I told you there is something you could do that would make you feel wonderful, would you be interested? If I told you it would cost little or no money and have you feeling like you were on the top of the world, would you give it a try? If I told you it could give you a longer, healthier life, would you have any reason not to do it? Now, if I told you it would help you find and maintain love in your life, would you listen? Well, I can promise you all of these and more. What is this incredible miracle? It's simple—doing something good for someone else. Research has shown that helping someone else can make you happier and healthier and help you live longer.

THE WAY IT WORKS

Giving to or helping others causes an endorphin release, much like the one that occurs during exercise. But instead of being called a "runner's high," the endorphin release that occurs as a result of helping others is called a "helper's high." People report experiencing health benefits of their own from helping others. One woman said she treated her stress-related headaches by shopping for clothing for poor children. Volunteer work at a nursing home keeps blood pressure under control for others.

Helping others does much more than decrease stress. Research has shown that helping others is personally fulfilling and can increase the self-esteem of the person providing the help. Most people studied by researchers said the beneficial feeling of helper's high returned later when they recalled helping others, increasing the benefits of each good deed.

One of the reasons many of us feel lonely is that we feel apart and separate from others. We look at the world and people around us and compare our own lives to theirs. Sometimes we compare favorably—we recognize we're better off than others—and so we may feel smug, self-satisfied, or at least "lucky." And sometimes we look around and see what others have and end up feeling "less than" or deprived. When we judge and compare, we are positioning ourselves on the outside looking in. We are not part of the world, not part of the human race; we feel disconnected, distant, separate, and sometimes desperately alone.

When we do something good for someone else, we form a bond of kindness. Kindness strengthens our soul. Through these acts we become part of the collective human experience. We are no longer separate; we become compassionate beings. When we help someone else, we actually help ourselves.

Study after study shows that altruism may be hard-wired into the human genome. Helping others actually has positive results for the one doing the helping. Helpful people experience more happiness, fewer strokes, and higher income. So helping others really is a win-win situation. You reap the intangible as well as the tangible benefits even as the person you are helping gets his or her needs met.

IT WORKS WHEN OTHER THINGS DON'T

Research shows that youth, brains, money, and looks are not all they're cracked up to be when it comes to making a person happy. Once the basic needs for food and shelter are met, additional material income does little to raise a person's satisfaction in life. A high IQ or an advanced education doesn't have much of a positive influence on happiness, either. A recent survey by the Centers for Disease Control and Prevention found that people ages twenty to twenty-four are sad for an average of

3.4 days a month, as opposed to just 2.3 days for people ages sixty-four to seventy-four.

In fact, a *Time* magazine poll on happiness discovered that helping others in need made people feel happier than playing with a pet, exercise, eating, or even having sex! Time after time, research and personal experience have shown that nothing makes a person feel as good as giving to another. Think of the difference between getting a present and giving one. Yes, it feels good to tear open the wrapping and discover what's inside that birthday or Christmas gift you've just been handed. But does it really compare with the excitement of selecting a present for someone else, picking the perfect wrapping paper, and signing the most suitable sentiment on just the right card? And how about those moments of anticipation while you watch them open the gift you so hope will please them? Those feelings, for me, dwarf anything produced by receiving a gift myself.

While I was on my personal retreat, Valentine's Day was coming up. I was beginning to feel sorry for myself. That "special one" would not be coming to my door with flowers and chocolates. There would be no romantic dinners or dreamily slow-dancing the night away. As Valentine's Day approached, I felt a dark cloud descending. I knew if I stayed home I would feel depressed. I was sure all my girlfriends would be calling the next day to tell me how wonderful their significant others were. I was beginning to feel unwanted, alone, and unloved.

I realized I had two choices. I could sit there and feel sorry for myself, or I could get out of myself. I could focus on what was missing in my life or on what was missing in someone else's.

It happened that I'd read an article about a group of homeless people who had gotten together as a way of protesting the lack of public housing. There was a vacant lot where the city had promised to build some. However, years had passed and the city still had not broken ground. It was a scandal, since the money set aside for the project was now missing. This meant that the project would be delayed indefinitely and the human hardships of the housing shortage would continue.

The homeless men and women had created a growing cardboard village, and it was making headlines. The news article told the story of the men, women, and even children who were living in these makeshift homes. The article grabbed my heart as it explained how these children lived without some of the most basic needs, such as running water. The article ended with a list of needed supplies. That was it! I could sit at home on Valentine's Day and feel sorry for what I was missing in my life—or I could get up and do something good for someone less fortunate than me.

A friend and I packed my truck with food, water, and needed supplies. I made some old-fashioned construction paper hearts to place on the items and headed down to the homeless village. We dropped off the stuff, complete with a Valentine's Day box of chocolates. The group was very happy to see us. I had an old tarp that someone had given me that had the paper hearts taped to it, wishing everyone a Happy Valentine's Day. A woman ran up and picked up the tarp. She was delighted as she gushed, "Oh, thank you…I needed a new roof!"

The gratitude I felt from the homeless people was immeasurable. A simple act of giving someone an old tarp that cost me nothing completely changed my day. I went home to my vacant apartment. There were still no chocolates, no flowers, and no man to sweep me off my feet. My apartment was empty, but I felt full. I had a warm glow that originated from inside me. I felt connected with the universe. I had done something good for someone else without any expectation for anything in return. But I did get a return, and it was much more than I could have ever bargained for. That simple act of human kindness made me feel wonderful. I believe that it also made one of those tiny, incremental changes in my picker that allowed me to see myself in a new and brighter light.

IT'S ABOUT LOVE

Giving to others is about love. We are learning to love and to give without expecting anything in return. The act of giving to others is sometimes called philanthropy. Philanthropy is derived from the Greek roots *phil*, which has to do with loving, and *antrop*, which pertains to mankind. Philanthropy literally means "loving mankind."

Giving to others strengthens our ability to love and be loved because we do it without fear of rejection. It makes it easier to love later, when we are in a relationship, because we have literally practiced and rewritten the limiting scripts that have led to our broken picker. We are practicing giving unconditionally so we can stop keeping score in our relationships. We can choose to give or not to give, but since it is unconditional, we stop attaching strings or qualifications. This fact is critical. If we are giving for recognition or some benefit other than the feeling we get from the act, then the conditions we are imposing defeat the purpose. Some people may choose to give anonymously to prevent this (easier to do with money or material donations, harder to do with personal volunteering, but possible). Others may want to keep reminding themselves that the feeling they receive by giving is payment in full, no matter how it is or isn't received.

The word "charity" is derived from the Latin word *caritas*, meaning "unconditional love." By giving to others we learn how it feels to give unconditionally, and we know that this kind of giving provides its own benefits, asking nothing in return from those to whom kindness is given.

GETTING STARTED

The beautiful part of this portion of your personal retreat program is that you don't have to be a humanitarian to reap the rewards of giving—something as simple as holding the door for another person can turn around their day. A smile over the produce bin can warm another shopper's heart. Letting another car into your lane during heavy traffic can bring gratitude.

Psychologists have been looking into some of the best ways to boost happiness. Their lists include visiting a nursing home, helping a friend's child with homework, mowing a neighbor's lawn, writing a letter to a grandparent. They note that doing five kind or caring acts a week, especially all in a single day, gives a measurable boost to the doer's sense of happiness.

A common practice among spiritual seekers and others who look to enlarge the presence of joy in their lives is to make a gratitude list. That can mean something as simple as taking a few minutes at bedtime to list at least five things you have been grateful for that day, and to do this over time, perhaps in a gratitude journal. Or it can be more elaborate, such as writing a testimonial thanking a teacher, pastor, or grandparent—anyone to whom you owe a debt of gratitude—and then visiting that person to read him or her the letter of appreciation. The remarkable thing is that people who do this just once report being happier and less depressed a month later.

Some things you can do include:

- Make that phone call to let someone know you are thinking about them.

- Bake some cookies and share them with everyone in the office.

- Put money in someone else's parking meter.

- Pay the road or bridge toll for the vehicle behind you.

- Give a dollar or more to the homeless man on the corner.

- Just smile at the next person you pass.

- Compliment someone on their shoes.

- Be courteous and helpful to other drivers.

- Allow the person behind you at the checkout counter to go first.

- Help someone pick up the change they just dropped.

- Relinquish that parking space instead of competing for it.

- Bring clean old towels or other needed supplies to the animal shelter.

- Volunteer at the local library to read to someone.

- Volunteer at a wildlife sanctuary.

- Hold the door for another person.

- Take a few minutes to talk to a stranger.

- Offer to share your umbrella in the rain.

- Bring food to a food bank.

- Drive someone home from a meeting or to an appointment.

- Give a friend a hug.

- Take someone out to lunch for no reason.

- Tell a sales clerk you appreciate him or her.

- Volunteer for an organization such as Habitat for Humanity and help build someone a new home.

- Volunteer at the local soup kitchen.

- Welcome a new neighbor.

- Offer to return the shopping cart for a harried mother.

- Bring a meal to a sick friend.

- Bring cookies to the fire station.

- Become a pen pal.

CONCLUSION

While doing something good for someone else is the definition of altruism, it pays great dividends by making you feel great. As a bonus, it can improve your self-esteem and help you live longer. It works whether you do good directly or anonymously. It benefits you as well as the person you help. It doesn't have to cost you a penny, and it increases your sense of prosperity. Finally, by doing something good for someone else you are learning one of the most valuable relationship skills you can possess—giving love unconditionally. Each giving act expands your choices and possibilities in ways you may never have imagined.

Activity:

♥ Do something good for someone else at least once a day.

CHAPTER TWELVE

Step Nine

Review of You

"THE UNEXAMINED LIFE IS NOT WORTH LIVING."

—SOCRATES

*E*very year as the crops come in, the farmer surveys his fields. He looks to see how his crops are doing, what's growing and what's not. He then does an evaluation of what his surveys tell him about his methods. What kinds of results did his efforts produce? Maybe he discovers that he needs to add more fertilizer or he needs better pest control. Maybe he has planted the wrong crop and needs to consider planting something completely different—peas instead of corn or maybe onions instead of soybeans. This examination is critical for maintaining a healthy and productive farm.

Like the farmer surveying his crops, each of us can benefit from careful analysis of what we are doing in our everyday lives. If we desire a healthy, purposeful life, we must periodically evaluate what is working and what's not. Then, like the farmer, we can make corrections so that we get maximum growth and harvest—and get rid of all the pests that are eating at us.

YOUR PERSONAL EVALUATION

Getting a realistic evaluation of your assets and liabilities is important. When we feel small and vulnerable, we may try to avoid looking at these feelings by defensive inflation, that is, by pumping up our own egos. We may become overly aggressive or bragging or argumentative. Sometimes we may try to make other people feel smaller by dominating a conversation, belittling, judging, or getting angry. Anger is a well-known way to deal with fear. Angry people often frighten us. But be assured that underneath the anger is someone who is afraid.

Another way to cope with feeling vulnerable is to hide. Sometimes we hide behind our titles or accomplishments. When someone asks, "Do you know who *I* am?" he or she is feeling small and needs to stand behind a title or a name in order to feel significant.

Women will sometimes try to compensate for feeling less than by dressing up. (*Feeling down? Dress up!*) They try to feel better by attracting the attention of others, usually men. I had a woman once tell me that her self-esteem was inversely proportional to her skirt length. If she wasn't feeling very confident, she tended to overcompensate by reaching for a miniskirt to draw the attention of male "admirers."

When we know ourselves well, we begin to develop healthy self-confidence based on who we really are. We don't have to rely on ego-inflated arrogance to protect or inflate ourselves. This arrogant behavior makes an intimate relationship with another person difficult, if not completely impossible. True intimacy requires knowing ourselves and finding peace with this knowledge. The peace comes from accepting all our parts, even the ones we may label as bad.

If a potential partner manages to look beyond our external, ego-inflated appearance to see "into" us, what will he see if all that is there is a false front put up to bolster our low level of self-confidence? Not the real woman within, that's for sure.

Your goal is to assess your strengths and weaknesses, which will in turn strengthen your self-confidence, so that in your personal relationships you no longer need to be afraid to let others see into you. You will know exactly what's inside yourself.

The following exercises are designed to help you assess your strengths and weaknesses. The goal of looking at your assets is to become more comfortable with yourself as you are—no more overinflating your importance or shrinking away from your true worth, but becoming just the right size and developing both confidence and humility. Through this process you'll find true peace within yourself so that you can more fully express yourself to another person. Remember, real intimacy requires full expression. When we develop healthy confidence with ourselves, we will be more attracted to, and more attractive to, healthy, confident men.

The goal of the review of your liabilities is to become more at ease with your perceived flaws and/or to change the things you want to change. You are going to look at the person you want to be and discover the parts that are not in line with that vision. You will then determine what corrective actions you want to take when you act in a way that is not in harmony with your chosen goals. You will learn the antidotes for your ill-fitting emotions or behaviors.

EXERCISE ONE

Let's begin by first looking at your perceived flaws. I say "perceived" because many times a flaw to one person is an asset to another. It all depends on how you look at it.

Imperfections

Each of us has liabilities. We each have things we would like to change. Some things we can change and others we must accept and learn to love in ourselves. Once we become comfortable with ourselves, we no longer look with disdain on our perceived negatives; instead, we choose to focus on maximizing our positives. Many great people have succeeded despite their limitations, or even, sometimes, because of them. Knowing about their problems makes their accomplishments even more rewarding.

Thomas Edison held a world record of 1,093 patents for inventions such as the electric light bulb and the phonograph. Yet Edison was almost totally deaf for most of his life. Instead of focusing on his disability, he decided to focus on his assets of analysis, organization, and creation.

Ludwig van Beethoven's hearing diminished to the point where during the premiere performance of his Ninth Symphony he had to be signaled to turn around in order to see that the audience was applauding. Eventually he went completely deaf, but continued to compose, conduct, and perform.

In the world of athletics, the longest field goal ever kicked is sixty-three yards. This was first done by Tom Dempsey, who was born without toes on his right foot (his kicking foot).

Edison once said, "If we did all the things we were capable of doing, we would literally astound ourselves."

It is by evaluating ourselves that we discover those astounding capabilities Edison speaks of.

Evaluation Exercise Instructions
Close your eyes. Breathe in and out, slowly allowing all the tension to leave your body. Relax your shoulders. Take deep, long breaths and allow your entire body to relax.

In the exercise that follows, there will be a list of questions to answer. Each time you need to ask yourself a question, close your eyes until an answer comes to your mind. Then open your eyes and jot down the answer. Repeat this for each question.

Evaluation Exercise
Imagine yourself sitting at an interview table with several other panelists (like the panel of judges on a TV talent show). About ten feet in front of your table is an empty chair. The room is dark, but there is a bright light illuminating the chair. You can see the people who will be interviewed, but they can't see you. The first person walks into the room and sits down. This is a person who loves you dearly and thinks you are just

perfect, or perhaps sees beyond any concepts of imperfection. This may be a grandmother, an old teacher, or a dear friend. They take the seat under the light. Someone from the panel of judges asks them to describe you. The judge asks the person in the seat:

"What makes her (meaning you) unique?"

You wait for an answer that comes to mind, imagining what this person might answer. Then you write down what they say. Then continue with the questions, always to the person in the chair, always about you.

"What are her special qualities?"

"How has she positively affected your life?"

Once again, wait for the answer that comes to you, imagining what this person might say, and then write it down.

Watch as they vividly describe you. Watch them smile as they describe your uniqueness. Listen to the stories of the value you have added to their lives.

Write it all down.

Thank that person and watch him or her leave the room.

Watch as the next person enters the room.

Watch as that person sits down, then looks up.

It is you. A panelist begins to ask you questions:

"What do you like about yourself?"

Write down your answer.

"What are your talents? Can you sing, dance, paint, stand on your head, or whistle? Can you play an instrument, touch your nose with your tongue, create shadow puppets, write a research paper, or finish a crossword puzzle?"

Write down all the answers, all the things you can do.

"What are the funny, quirky things about you?"

Write them down.

"What qualities are you most proud of?"

Write them down.

"What would you say is your best quality?"

Write it down.

"What are your favorite things to do?"

Make a list of all the things you like to do. Do you like to backpack, play video games, listen to comedy, or read books? This also will provide you with a list of things you might have in common with another person, for when you begin dating.

"What are the accomplishments you're most proud of? Did you win the spelling bee in third grade? Did you bake an awesome pumpkin pie last year for Thanksgiving? Can you cook?"

"What else would you like to put on the list?"

Write it down.

"What do you dislike about yourself?"

Write it down.

"What would you like to change about yourself?"

Write it down.

"What are the mistakes you made in your past relationships that you don't want to repeat in your next one?"

Write them down.

"If you had the opportunity to live your life over again, what would you do differently?"

Write it down.

After you have finished writing, thank yourself, and imagine getting up and leaving the chair under the light.

Take out another sheet of paper to get ready for the next interview. Watch as the next interviewee enters. It's your last boyfriend. Close your eyes and listen as one of the other panelists asks him to describe your relationship.

When he describes you, what does he say he most loved about you?

Write it down.

"What did she do that made you laugh?"

Write it down.

"What would you say are her greatest assets?"

Write them down.

Now listen to him as he describes what he didn't like about you.

Write those things down.

What are the things that, in his opinion, would have made you a better partner? Remember, it is your job to listen. Do not try to defend yourself or make excuses; just listen to what he has to say as objectively as you can.

Write these items down.

Write down the habits of yours that annoyed him.

Now, write down the behavior that you did not like about yourself when you were with him.

Write it all down.

Thank him and watch him leave the room.

Now you are ready to evaluate the information you have received in this exercise.

EVALUATION

Take a look at your list. Begin by folding a piece of paper (standard 8½" × 11" paper is fine) the long way, down the center, so that you have two columns. At the top of the left column you will write the word "Assets"; on top of the right column you will write the word "Liabilities." Your asset column should contain all your positive qualities, anything and everything that you like about yourself. In the liabilities column write down all the things you don't like about yourself.

Once you have completed these lists, take one more look. Sometimes something you perceive as an imperfection can actually become an asset. It all depends on how you look at it. For instance, I once went for a job interview to which I had to bring my school transcripts. I felt a sense of shame as I reluctantly handed over the papers. I stammered as I tried to explain my academic dismissal, which appeared in the middle of my undergraduate transcript. My interviewer patiently listened as I painfully tried to explain away my humiliation. As I droned on, he started to laugh. I was mortified, but then he said, "I can tell you're worried about what I think of your academic dismissal." He then said something that I would have never guessed he would say. He said, "You should be proud of this," pointing to my blemished transcript. My mouth dropped open as he continued: "Most people would have given up at this defeat, but this shows me you don't give up. This indicates that you have character and tenacity. Instead of accepting failure you picked yourself up and tried again."

Wow, I never looked at it that way. He was right. I hadn't given up. I went back and finished my degree and even went on to graduate school.

After that day, whenever I went on an interview I proudly passed over my transcripts, and even said, "May I point out my academic dismissal?"

Our greatest failures can be our greatest successes; it all depends on how we look at them. Review your sheet. Is there anything you can move to your assets list, if you look at it differently? Since we are often our own worst critics, it can be useful to look at ourselves as the others in our lives see us. We can get a different perspective on both our flaws (as I did during the interview) and our assets.

Did any of your errors or flaws result in you learning something valuable? We often learn more from our mistakes than from our successes. Is there anything that you have written down as a liability that you learned a valuable lesson from? If so, move that one to your asset list. Be grateful for the lesson and consider it a small price for the education.

Look over your list. Can you find any value in your life for those things you perceive as defects? If it wasn't for one of the greatest errors in history, you might not be living here. Christopher Columbus was looking for a way to the riches of the Indies, not a New World. His greatest mistake ended up becoming a great asset, for him and many others.

Once you complete this part of the assignment, take another look at your liabilities column. Carefully review your list, and place next to each item a word that best represents the underlying emotion associated with that behavior.

When you are done, take a look at which emotion showed up the most. Was it jealousy? Which emotion did you find the most embarrassing? Your list provides you with a blueprint for creating the person you want to be. Now that you have identified the emotions that plague you, you are free to change them if you wish. Once again, each of these steps is helping to change and improve your picker, providing you with a much clearer picture of what is truly available for you.

Changing behaviors we don't like about ourselves takes discipline and practice. When you practice a behavior, it becomes more a part of you.

Conversely, if you stop practicing or disassociate with the behavior, you become free of it. (Use it or lose it.) You can begin to extinguish a problem behavior by not engaging in it and by avoiding all stimuli that would prompt you to engage in that behavior.

Some behaviors are so ingrained that we hardly realize we are doing them. In order for us to disassociate from them we must first become more cognizant of the behavior, and then work on changing it. I once heard of a man who tried to give up swearing. He made a deal with his grown son that every time his son heard him swear, he would give him a dollar. After realizing he was quickly becoming poor, he began to change his behavior.

I want to be a loving, sweet, and kind person. However, when I did my own evaluation, I realized that quite often I acted in a manner that was petty, jealous, and loathsome. My belief in scarcity would manifest itself in this detestable behavior. If I sensed a threat, I would become scared. This fear caused me to make snide remarks, or sometimes recoil and sulk. The results were always the same; I was uncomfortable and unhappy, and that energy was felt by the people around me. I desperately wanted to change this.

By examining ourselves objectively, we can see what we wish to improve. Looking at ourselves and becoming the best person we can be eliminates our need to blame others or point our finger at life's situations. We can calmly take responsibility for ourselves and make changes when necessary.

THE ANTIDOTE

In the second column of the table on page 137 you will find the antidote to your toxic emotions. When you begin to feel that emotion, respond by performing the action that is opposite it. For example, when you feel jealousy, instead of sulking or becoming upset, you react with trust. When you act with trust, you don't overreact; you go along believing you are safe and that everything is happening for your higher good.

When you first begin to respond in a different manner, it will feel awkward and unnatural, maybe even "phony." But with continued practice, you will begin to feel a shift in your own attitude. Over time you will move from acting to feeling. There is an old saying that goes, "You can act your way into a new way of thinking, but you can't think your way into a new way of acting." That means that when you start, you will not be feeling it, but over time you will. You will "fake it until you make it," as people sometimes say. There's nothing wrong with faking it, but of course, eventually, you have to make it.

For example, once I had to pick up my boyfriend at the airport. However, as I jumped on the highway, I was quickly met with a traffic jam. Looking at the clock, I began to get angry. I was going to be late picking him up, and I didn't want him waiting. I began trying to swerve in and out of lanes, jockeying for the best position. Other drivers were becoming irritated, honking their horns and swerving also. At one point I cut sharply to fill an empty space in one of the lanes ahead. At the same time I was cutting over, a car was speeding up. We were both fighting for this small piece of asphalt. I had a decision to make. I could continue on my manic struggle or I could meet my growing anger with patience. I decided to back off. I couldn't change the traffic jam, but I could change the way I was responding to it. I decided to sit back and pop in a CD I had been meaning to listen to. As soon as I relaxed, the traffic jam dissipated and I passed the troubled area. I arrived at the airport on time and in a loving, happy mood. I was the person I wanted to be.

Make a plan of action for change. Talk to your friends for support and suggestions. Then implement your course of action.

If You Feel	Respond With
Angry	Peace
Apprehensive	Courage
Boastful	Humility
Critical	Gentleness
Competitive	Cooperation
Controlling	Allowing (let go)
Depressed	Cheer
Dishonest	Trustworthiness
Gluttonous	Moderation
Gossipy	Temperance
Greedy or Selfish	Giving
Judgmental	Tolerance
Mean or Jealous	Kindness
Nagging or Manipulative	Support
Negative	Positivity
Overemotional	Emotional stability
Procrastinating	Diligence
Resistant to growth	Willingness
Regretful or Self-pitying	Acceptance
Resentful	Forgiveness
Discontented	Gratitude

GRATITUDE

I ended the table with the word "gratitude." Becoming grateful for everything in life, the good and the bad, can be transformative. Viewing life through this lens, we are no longer its victims, pushed around by the ebbs and flows. When we are grateful we become active participants. We realize we have choices, even if the choice is just whether to be grateful or not. Sometimes, of course, gratitude requires some faith—belief that time will ultimately reveal the reason that we should be grateful.

Some of you may be saying to yourself, "Yes, but my situation is different. You don't understand what I had to go through," or "How can I be grateful for _____?"

Viktor Frankl was an Austrian neurologist and psychiatrist prior to World War II. On September 25, 1942, he, his wife, and his parents were shipped off to the Theresienstadt concentration camp. Later he would be moved to Auschwitz, the concentration camp most infamous for its brutality and suffering and the death of thousands of people. During their internment, Frankl's wife and parents were killed. After he was liberated, he wrote:

"We who lived in concentration camps can remember the men who walked through huts comforting others, giving away their last piece of bread. They may have been few in number, but they offer sufficient proof that everything can be taken from a man but one thing: the last of human freedoms—to choose one's attitude in any given set of circumstances."[4]

Frankl took these lessons into the world for the rest of his life—living proof that we can choose to be grateful.

ACCEPTANCE

Your list of things you would love to be able to change about yourself may contain items that are difficult to be grateful for. For these items we will begin with acceptance. When we can accept the good and bad parts of ourselves, we can look the world in the eye with quiet self-assurance. When we know in our heart that we are each a child of God, a unique being with purpose and self-worth, we will be ready to take our place in the dance of life.

---

4   *Man's Search for Meaning* by Viktor Frankl. Copyright © 1959, 1984, 1992 by Viktor E. Frankl. Reprinted by permission of Beacon Press, Boston.

To work on acceptance, I had to work on my faith. I had to believe that things happened for a reason (although I might not be privy to the reason). I had to come to believe that things happened for my ultimate good. So when I lost a boyfriend, I reminded myself that it wasn't because God hated me. It was because it was for my ultimate good. I was growing from the experience. And it was making room in my life for someone better suited for me. In fact, the experience of being rejected was helping to prepare me for that person.

People admire others who can accept themselves just the way they are. We call them "down-to-earth" or "genuine" or "real." People who can accept themselves just as they are fulfill their purpose with what they have been given in life, and they do it with confidence and pride.

Now let's take a look at what's left—the asset side of your list. This should be a wonderful cornucopia of unique qualities.

YOUR UNIQUENESS LIST

Your asset list is going to become your uniqueness list. We turn to this list to celebrate our individuality. Each of us has a role to play in the universe. We were each born with a unique set of traits designed to allow us to play that role. The list of these traits is the blueprint for your life.

When you are feeling down, review this list, relish what you have, and celebrate your assets. When you are tempted to look at what you don't have, look at what you do have and be grateful. Know that you are worthy and loved. Your gratitude for what you have will release your feelings of inadequacy and lack.

Each of us has unique attributes. Each of us has special gifts, and each of us plays a different role in the universe. We sometimes forget this. We look at other people and feel envious because we are so sure our lives would be better if we only were as pretty as this one, or as young as that one, or that we had the other one's money…and the list goes on.

Envy is a symptom of a lack of appreciation for our own uniqueness and self-worth. When we discount our own attributes in this way, we diminish our power and literally rob the world of what we have to give. We each have our own special light. Your challenge is to recognize it and share it with the world.

Your uniqueness list will become very important when you begin dating. We all have times when we must remind ourselves that we are unique, and treat ourselves with respect and love.

Activity:

- ♥ Conduct your evaluation.

- ♥ Review both of your lists.

- ♥ Repeat this affirmation frequently: "I accept and I am grateful for all parts of me. They make me uniquely qualified to be me."

CHAPTER THIRTEEN

Step Ten

Dreamweaving

"ALL THAT WE SEE OR SEEM
IS BUT A DREAM WITHIN A DREAM."

—EDGAR ALLAN POE

*I*n this section we are going to have fun. This part is all about dreaming. Your activity for this section is to daydream; dream and dream big. Dream about anything and everything you want or could want in your life, and when you are done, dream a little more.

WHAT IS DAYDREAMING?

Daydreaming is the visualization of dreamlike images while you are awake. It may be revisiting past experiences or thinking about the future. Daydreamers become temporarily unaware of their surroundings, and their eyes usually hold a blank stare.

Daydreaming sometimes gets a bad rap. In school, your teacher may have even become annoyed with you for daydreaming. At work, you might actually get in trouble for daydreaming. Daydreamers are frequently considered unproductive and lazy. (But not here!)

WHY DAYDREAMING IS IMPORTANT

Arthur Fry liked to sing in his church choir. One day, as the pastor began the sermon, Arthur Fry drifted off into a daydream. One of the little scraps of paper that he used to mark his place in the hymnbook fell out and fluttered to the floor. As Arthur watched the paper floating to the floor, he thought, "What I really need is a little bookmark that will stick to the page but will not tear the paper when I remove it." Fortunately, Arthur had a colleague who had been working on a temporary adhesive. Arthur's little daydreaming thought, together with a bit of ingenuity, would later become the yellow sticky note, one of the most successful office products of all time.

History is full of stories in which inventors uncovered major breakthroughs while daydreaming. Sir Isaac Newton, whose musings on gravity while daydreaming under an apple tree led to what we know as Newtonian physics, is considered the greatest mathematician who ever lived, and his research laid the groundwork for the theory of relativity.

Albert Einstein, an intellectual descendant of Newton, is also famous for his use of daydreaming. The theory of relativity resulted from his daytime visualization. Inventors and scientists are not the only ones who use daydreams. Olympic athletes and performers use this kind of daydreaming, or visualization, to enhance their physical performance as well as their will to win, imagining themselves practicing, competing, and winning repeatedly, so that their brains lead them through their routines and performances flawlessly in actual competition.

HOW TO DAYDREAM

Most of us already know how to daydream, though we may not allow ourselves to do it for fear that it's unproductive or a waste of our time. However, in this exercise we are going to let our imaginations run wild in a very special way.

Start by finding a quiet place where you will not be interrupted, maybe the hammock in the backyard, the swing on the porch, or a comfy rocking chair. If you would like, get a cup of tea. Maybe you'd prefer to daydream while sitting in a warm bubble bath. You want to find a place where you can comfortably stay for an hour, if needed. Bring a pen and paper.

Get comfortable, in any position you prefer. Clear your mind and focus only on what you are about to read below.

Take several deep breaths, releasing the tension from your shoulders. As the tension begins to dissipate from your body, close your eyes. Now, begin to picture your perfect life in your mind's eye. Allow these images to play like a movie in your imagination. See your home, your family, your car, your clothes, some of your personal possessions, or even a lack of them, if that's your wish. Now picture your friends. Picture what you want to do in an average day. Picture your job(s) and your hobbies. Picture your life.

What does that life include? Picture yourself first getting up in the morning, how you spend your time during the day, people you are with, places you go, the activities you most enjoy.

Do you work? In your daydreams, what would be your ideal job? Is it the same as the job you now have? If not, how is it different? Maybe you don't have a job at all—then how do you spend your time?

Do you have children in your daydream? What are their genders? Their ages? How do they delight you? What other things about them bring you pleasure? How do they displease you?

Where do you live? What is your home like? Do you live in a house, a loft, a condo, or a tree house? Maybe you don't envision a home at all; maybe you are traveling in an RV or on a sailboat, or camping out in the rain forest.

If you have a home, what color is it? What is its architectural style? How old is it? What does it look like inside? Picture the furniture, the colors of walls, any artwork. Describe your favorite room in this house. Why is it your favorite room?

Do you have a yard? What does the yard look like? Is it planted with flowers, or maybe vegetables? Do you have large trees, or maybe a pond? Maybe you have taken up organic gardening or herb gardening. What are your favorite items and why are they special?

How about pets? How many? What kind? Can you name them?

Do you have a car? What kind? What color?

Now picture yourself. What do you look like? How are you dressed? Does the way you dress indicate the lifestyle that you want?

Keep dreaming, imagining anything and everything in your life—even what's in the cupboards and pantry if it seems important to you. When you find yourself smiling or even laughing, jot down the image that inspired that feeling.

The goal here is to daydream in as much detail as possible. Keep thinking about what you want in your life, how you want your life to be on a day-to-day basis. Your ideas may change as the days go on. That's fine. We are creating a life just like we would create a painting, one stroke at a time. Some artists say that they rarely begin with a finished vision of their paintings but that the image evolves as the paint is applied and the beauty emerges. As you open up your imagination and allow yourself to dream, more and more thoughts and images will arise in your consciousness. Your first thoughts may be ideas of a way of life that someone else suggested to you. It may include images of what other people told you a good life should be. That's okay. Your goal is to allow the images to flow until you reach your true heart's desire.

You may already have clear images of your heart's desire. Or maybe you have a vague idea of what it is but are afraid to dream it. Sometimes we don't allow our dreams to surface for fear of losing them or being disappointed. The irony is that if we don't allow them to come to the surface, we have already lost them—and they need to be revived. No dream is too small or too big. All things are possible. Many children dream of becoming president of the United States, and some folks make it. Barack Obama or Bill Clinton could have easily been accused of dreaming too big.

SMALL BEGINNINGS

As you begin with your dream life, choose one small thing from the dream of your heart's desire that you can bring into your life right now. I watched this transformation occur in my friend Jana. For years she had a subsistent life; it seemed like whenever she got a little money, something would break that required her to spend that little extra. It was one thing after another; she lost her job, she wrecked her car, then her cat got sick. She never seemed to get ahead. She avoided buying anything extra, purchasing only what she needed.

Finally, Jana decided to put the dream life idea into action. She decided she wanted to live life more creatively. Although she didn't have much money, she decided to buy a watercolor set and paper anyway. She began doing watercolors and included some decoupage. Soon her apartment was full of creative works. The entire energy of the place changed—it had become alive. Her demeanor also changed; the old shrinking violet was now coming into full bloom.

One day she called me and said, "I have decided to move." I was surprised because her apartment was now starting to look so beautiful, decorated as it was with her artistry. More importantly, she had just started a new job and I was wondering if it was financially prudent for her to do this. She explained that her old apartment represented lack. She said, "I stayed there mostly because it was furnished, but it was noisy, making it hard to sleep. The life I want does not include a noisy apartment and someone else's stuff.

A few weeks later, I helped her move her new furniture into a beautiful, spacious, quiet apartment that backed up to a nature preserve. In the morning she would sit on her balcony and watch egrets fish. Eventually, other parts of her life began to transform. After years of wanting but not finding a relationship, she met someone. She left that second apartment to live with her fiancé and is now living another dream—going back to school. And it all began with a watercolor set.

Activity:

- Dream of the life you want. Set aside a little time every day this week just to create the daydream of life. When you find something you particularly like, write it down.

- Just keep dreaming, and allow the dreams to expand on themselves each day. At the end of this week, write down your ideal life.

- If it takes longer, that's fine. Just know that everything in our lives starts with our dreams.

- Then, make one small move toward that dream.

CHAPTER FOURTEEN

Step Eleven
Plan-a-Man:
Build Your Beau

"SHE WHO FAILS TO PLAN, PLANS TO FAIL."
—ANONYMOUS

*H*ere is where we will build your man. That's right; you are going to MANufacture your ideal guy. No, we aren't talking about building a Frankenstein-like creature from bits and pieces of different men. This is where you sit down and write everything you want in your next man. You can have your heart's desires, but you first have to figure out what your heart's desires are.

WHY PLAN-A-MAN?

Have you ever gone to the grocery store hungry and without a list? I have. I ended up with a cart full of items, but many of them were things I didn't really need or want. To make matters worse, when I got home I realized I had forgotten essentials like bread and coffee. Instead, I had bags and bags of snacks and munchies that looked good at the time, but now I wanted something more substantial.

I am sure this happens to everyone from time to time. You have an idea of what you want, but you become distracted by all the options. Dating can be a lot like going shopping hungry. Without a clear idea, you end up with something that looked like it would taste good at the time, but when you get it home you realize you forgot what you'd set out to get in the first place.

In the past you may have never really considered what was important to you. You would end up with a man who really didn't fit—and you didn't understand why. By sitting down and carefully planning what you want, you will be able to spot it when it shows up.

WHAT IS PLAN-A-MAN?

Plan-a-man is a brainstorming activity. You will generate a list of assets and characteristics you would like in a man. Once the list is generated, you will then categorize your items according to their importance to you. This will be your road map to help you in the dating process. It's similar to a business plan. If you want a successful business, most people would agree, it would be crazy not to have a plan. Why should choosing a life partner be less important than starting a business? Your man-plan will provide you with the basic requirements. You can attract what you want once you know what you want.

HOW TO BUILD A BEAU

In order to complete this section, find a quiet place where you will not be interrupted for at least half an hour. Find a place where you can sit down comfortably and relax. Be sure that you have a pen and paper.

Close your eyes and take several deep breaths. When you open your eyes, write down a word or a brief description of your perfect man. Be creative as well as practical. Write down as much as you can without thinking about it too much. Make a long list. Think of as many things as possible, and don't be shy.

Let me help you begin. How about starting with "single and available"? We are not going to date "potential." If he is not single and available, then you will take a pass. Next, write down what you like. If you want a man who cleans the house, write it down. If you want a poet, or someone who loves to cook, write it down.

Write down lifestyle desires. If you want someone who shares your passions, write it down. If you like to snow ski, write it down. Write down hobbies and activities—his and yours, if you want him to share them. If you want someone who loves to dance, write it down. You don't have to find someone who is an accomplished ballroom dancer, but write down someone who is at least willing to try. If you are a cat lover, you probably do not want to date someone who is allergic. Write that down, too.

Write down as many things as you can think of, as fast as you think of them. Don't worry about editing yourself; you will do that later. Just get as many things on paper as you can. You will want a long list to work with, so the more you have, the better. Let all possibilities tumble out of your mind and onto the page.

Do you want a family man? Do you want someone who wants children? How about someone who already has children? Do you want someone who can make you laugh? Would you prefer a serious-minded intellectual? How about rough and rugged? Do you like the strong, silent type, or someone who commands the room? Or would you prefer someone supportive, while you command the room?

What do you want physically? Do you prefer short, tall, fat, or thin? What about his hair? If he has hair, what color? What about facial hair, knuckle hair, and back hair?

Do you prefer someone who drives a Volvo or pickup truck, a BMW or a Harley-Davidson?

What about religion? Do you want someone who is Christian, Jewish, spiritual, Buddhist, or an atheist? Do you prefer someone who is open and inclusive, or maybe a little cynical? Hometown boy or metropolitan man?

What about money? Do you want someone financially secure? If given a choice between someone who works many hours but has lots of money and someone who has less money but more time to play, which would you choose?

What about types of work, lifestyles, and personal values? Do you prefer someone who works with his hands or with his mind? Do you like city dwellers or cowboys? I have included a list of characteristics you may want to consider:

Funny	Serious	Laid-back
Driven	Good-hearted	Successful
Old-fashioned	Family man	Jet-setter
Homebody	Adventurous	Dependable
Rugged	Neat	Stylish
Professional	Strong	Brawny
Cultured	Bald	Hairy
Big	Thin	Affectionate
Stoic	Talkative	Stable
Risk taker	Candid	Diplomatic
Direct	Cautious	Spontaneous
Biker	Athletic	Banker
Cute	Average	Kind
Reclusive	Likes animals	No animals
Sense of humor	Business-minded	Creative
Open to learning	Positive	Type A
Type B	Dominant	Submissive
Cooks	Likes your cooking	Likes to clean
Hearty eater	Vegetarian	Likes to travel
Likes to stay home	Independent	Codependent
Drinks	Doesn't drink	Likes to (activity)
Romantic	High-tech	Low-tech
Likes to read	Prefers TV	Likes mountains
Likes the shore	Listens	Thoughtful
Owns a tie	Works in boots	Charming
Intelligent	Smokes	Doesn't smoke
Decisive	Open to change	Nerdy

Do you drink? If you consider yourself a wine connoisseur and like to travel to Napa Valley once a year, then a relationship with a recovering alcoholic is probably not a good idea.

Write down as many things as you can think of. The list can also suggest other characteristics to you. Sometimes it can be difficult to figure out exactly what you want. It can be easier to figure out what you don't want. For example, I don't want an ax murderer, I don't want a cheater, and I don't want someone who is messy. Go ahead and write all those down.

Once you are done, you are going to review the list. It is preferable to change any negatives to positive. So instead of writing, "I don't want a cheater," write, "I want someone who is trustworthy and honest." Instead of saying, "I don't want someone who is messy," say, "I want someone who is neat and tidy."

Now that you have your list together, look it over. Have you forgotten anything? Have you neglected to put down something you feel is impossible? If you want someone who loves to give pedicures, write it down. Write down anything and everything you could possibly want in a man. Remember, you must conceive before you achieve.

PRIORITIZING YOUR LIST

The next task is to prioritize. You have an idea about what you want, but right now all the characteristics you've written down are weighted pretty much equally. For example, maybe it seemed obvious at the moment that "likes my kids" is much more important than "stylish dresser," but since they are now just lumped together, there is no way of telling them apart.

Why Is Prioritizing Important?

You have an opportunity to write the script for your heart's desires. Not only are you telling the universe what you want, you are also creating a type of checklist. When you are dating, you are bombarded with many different opportunities. You need to prioritize in order of importance. Not all things are equal; some are very important while others are "nice to have" but really not important at all. For example, it would be nice to have someone who knew how to build a website, but since I can easily hire someone to do that for me, it's just not that important.

I once had a friend who was very excited about a man she had just met. She started to tell me all the great assets he possessed. She gushed, "And he plays the guitar, so we can play together." I couldn't remember her ever playing the guitar, so I had to ask the obvious. "Do you play?" She grinned sheepishly. "Well, no, but I would like to one day." Obviously, duet guitar playing should not be top priority if you don't play.

Without a prioritized list, you walk into a date thinking you know what you want, but the next thing you know you get blindsided by hormones. You think, "Okay, I know he's a Merchant Marine and I want a man who is home every night, but damn, he's so cute. Maybe…we could work something out." Without a clear set of priorities it becomes much easier to get swayed by a charming smile. Your body likes him, but is he the best choice for you, given the bigger picture? Your list will tell you.

How to Prioritize

Look over your list and make a mark next to the characteristics that are the most important to you. Don't worry about being silly or shallow. If long hair on a guy is really important to you, make a mark next to it. Mark everything you believe you cannot live without. Remember, this is your list, this is your truth. If you only date lawyers because everyone in your family marries a lawyer, but you really want to date a musician, then write down the musician. This is your desire, regardless of any family traditions or social biases.

As you mark your priorities you will find that there are a few that you would like but that are not that important. If you wrote down "loves tennis" but you only play once a year, then that one is probably not terribly important to you.

I have included a chart with four categories. The categories are Must Have, Would Like, Negotiable, and Deal Breaker. Take all the ones you placed a mark next to that you felt were most important and list them in the Must Have column.

Next, take the rest of the list and place each characteristic in either Would Like or Negotiable. The Would Like category is for things that you want but that are not Must Haves. For example, I would like a man with dark hair, but if Johnny Depp went bald, I probably wouldn't turn him away.

The Would Like differs from the Negotiable in that the Negotiable is purely optional. For example, it would be nice to date someone who liked to snow ski, but since I live in Florida and I have not been on skis for more than seven years, snow skiing would be negotiable.

After you've prioritized your list in this way, most of your man's characteristics should be in the Would Like or Negotiable column. In fact, there should be no more than ten items in the Must Have column. If you have more than ten, your requirements are too stringent. Look over your Must Have column for items that you can move into another column. Must Haves are important, but you can have so many that no one could ever possibly meet the requirements. Take a look at the sample priority chart below, and then use the blank sample underneath to make your own priority chart.

Must Have	Would Like	Negotiable	Deal Breaker
Single, available	A white-collar job	Likes to travel	Racist
Moral values	Churchgoer	My denomination	Felon
Own transportation	A Harley	Tattoos	Facial tattoos
Own hair	Dark and wavy hair	Sparse hair	Bad toupee
Excellent hygiene	Smells like the woods	Clean-shaven	Bad hygiene
Music lover	Rock musician	Enjoys live concerts	Hates music
A love of reading	Same favorite author as me	Reads news magazines	Illiterate
Great sense of humor	Makes me laugh	Likes funny movies	Laughs at me

Must Have	Would Like	Negotiable	Deal Breaker

Too rigid a list of requirements is a defense mechanism. If no one can meet your requirements, they you get to reject that person first, thereby saving yourself from being the one who gets rejected. Although this might protect you from the pain of rejection, it also prevents you from ever developing a healthy relationship. Therefore, limit your Must Have column to ten items or fewer.

Once you decide where each item goes, fill in the appropriate columns in the table. The final column is the Deal Breaker column, which we will work on next.

DEAL BREAKERS

Deal breakers are nonnegotiable, undesirable qualities. These are the qualities that, if possessed by the other person, make pursuit of a relationship out of the question. A man who is married or living with someone else would be a deal breaker for me. Deal breakers are different for different people. What may be an asset to you is a deal breaker for someone else. If you love to travel, then a relationship with an airline pilot may be ideal; however, if you are terrified of the thought of yourself or anyone else you know flying, then a relationship with an airline pilot would cause you an intolerable amount of anxiety.

Determining your deal breakers before entering a relationship can save you great sorrow and possibly years of regret. It you want to have children, dating someone who hates being around children could easily end in heartache. We have to take the person as he is. We can't think that we will change him. If he doesn't want kids, no amount of bringing him around your friend's cute and cuddly babies is going to change that.

Of course, don't make your deal breakers too strict. There are many happy relationships where the two people involved appear to be opposites. Take, for example, James Carville and Mary Matalin, polar opposites at work on the political front, he a Democratic strategist and she a Republican advisor. Yet when they go home, they put their political views aside, as evidenced by their marriage since 1993.

The clearer you can make your priorities in this list, the better. You can have your heart's desires, but you first must be clear about those desires. When you are specific and thorough with your table, you will find it easier to choose from the many options you will be presented with while dating.

Your table may change as you date. You may meet men with characteristics that you didn't think of or didn't think you could find. There may be a combination of traits that you just didn't think you could find in the same individual. For example, I knew a man who worked a construction crane by day, but danced ballet in his off time. I would never have come up with that combination by myself. You are going to find that you can have what you want. By making this list, you are telling the universe what you want, which makes it easier for it to provide it for you.

Activity:

- Take your time and thoughtfully complete the list of what you want in your life partner. If you like, talk with other people about what they want in a life partner. Consider what they have to say. Don't speed through the process—carefully consider each item until you feel really good about your choice. Then set the list down for a few days.

- After a few days, look at the list again. Is there anything on it you want to change? Did you forget something, or realize that a characteristic that was important when you wrote it down is just not that important now? Make the appropriate changes. This is the best fit for you.

CHAPTER FIFTEEN

Step Twelve
Making a Vision Board

"VISION WITHOUT ACTION IS A DAYDREAM.
ACTION WITHOUT VISION IS A NIGHTMARE."
—JAPANESE PROVERB

*N*ow that you have reached this point, you should have a firm understanding of what you want in your life and in your relationship. In this next activity, we are taking all those bits and pieces and creating a "vision board," or "life board." This board will be a visual representation of your desires. In order to manifest your desires, you must picture them clearly. That is what this chapter is all about—gaining clarity and a vision for your life.

You can be as simple or as creative as you would like with this. The basic ingredients include a poster board, several magazines, scissors, and glue. Find magazines that represent you. Choose ones that have the feel you like and contain activities you enjoy. The vision board, with the images you choose, is a powerful tool, so you want to choose your images carefully.

While I was working on my first vision board, I went to the library for magazines. They had a stack of old magazines that were on sale for a nickel apiece. Most didn't resonate with me, but they had a few surfing magazines that I purchased. (A major 20¢ investment!) I cut out several pictures of couples embracing, symbolizing the type of affectionate relationship I wanted. Since these were surfing and water-related magazines, I ended up with pictures of couples on the beach and on boats. There were also several action-type pictures such as waterskiing and people on jet skis.

I was amazed by how accurate my board turned out to be. The man I fell in love with—in real life—ended up being a yacht broker. On our second date he invited me to fly to the Keys with him and spend the day sailing back to Fort Lauderdale on a yacht. Since then we have had many boating adventures, and I often reflect back to the serendipity of finding those nickel magazines.

We are going to start by cutting out piles of pictures. You can get pictures anywhere. If you can't find what you are looking for with the media you have available, then search the Internet. Find images of what you desire and print them out. Just keep cutting and piling. We are not going to paste to our board just yet.

What you may discover is that your first choice may not be your best. But it may inspire you to explore that desire further. One picture may lead to another, which leads to another, and so on until you really have what you want. For example, you may decide on a particular dream home. You may find pictures of a home you like. Later you may be flipping through a magazine and find a picture of something you did not think of—maybe a unique feature or a pool or garden. You could start out in a modest apartment and end up in a sprawling mansion. That's okay. Remember, you cannot achieve it until you dream it.

We are going to collect piles of pictures and narrow them down later. Collect pictures of all your desires. Choose images that represent trips you would like to take. Cut out pictures of hobbies you would like to do. Select images of the body you want, new shoes, or maybe a new car. Make sure you have a mixture of all facets of your life. What do you want for a future career? Where do you want to live? Do you want children? How about health or wealth? Nothing is out of the realm of possibilities. Remember, all desires are God-given, and there is nothing to be ashamed of. When we get in touch with our true desires, we are tapping into the universal power. Many times we censor ourselves by saying things like "That will never happen" or "That is foolish." This inhibits our own ability to conceptualize and work toward our truest desires.

We are given the desires and the tools to create our lives. When we slow down enough to listen to what our soul wants, we can find our truest desires in life. This is usually different from what our head wants. Our head is usually competitive; it likes to have more than others. Your head, or ego, usually wants to be better-looking, faster, and wealthier than others. When you find yourself feeling competitive, then you are not tapping into your true desire. In addition, if you find yourself wanting something because someone else believes it is good for you, you are not tapping into your truest desire. If your family wants you to be a doctor because family members from every generation before you were doctors, but you are reluctant, that reluctance is frequently your soul trying to be heard.

I knew I wanted to be a writer, so I cut out a picture of a book. But looking at the little book, that goal seemed rather small. So I decided to dream bigger. Next, I found a picture of a pile of money and a banner that said "best-seller." That was looking better, but I thought, "Still not good enough." Finally, I got on the Internet and pulled up a picture of Oprah Winfrey's stage, complete with Oprah sitting on her couch getting ready to interview me. Now my vision was perfect.

After you have collected your box full of pictures, you are going to review them. You want to spread them out on a large, open space, a large table or maybe the floor. Spread them all out so you can see them. After they are all spread out, close your eyes. Sit silently for a moment and take several deep breaths. Then ask yourself what your truest desires are. Open your eyes and look around. What image does your gaze linger on first? Pick that one up. Continue to look around at all the pictures. Does one make you smile? Pick that one up. Go through all the clippings, selecting the ones that make you smile or that you feel drawn to. Make sure you balance out your life. Select pictures that represent your job, home, relationships, and hobbies. Once you have narrowed your selection down, you are going to paste these images on your board.

Begin with that first image you selected. Pick this one up again. Ask yourself if this represents a central theme in your life or something you want most. If the answer is yes, then place that in the center of your board. If not, choose a more appropriate image for the center. Then continue to paste the rest of the selected pictures on the board. Don't worry if you have gaps. You don't want to make it too cluttered because then it will be difficult to understand. Once you have pasted in all the pictures you want, review the board. Is there anything you missed? If you are satisfied with your board, you are ready for the next step.

Now that you know what you want, you need to manifest it. Earlier you learned about the "ohm" meditation. Now you are going to use the "ah" meditation, which has been described as the manifesting meditation. As with our earlier meditation, you are going to say the word to help you focus and remove extraneous thoughts. The difference now is that instead of focusing on your breathing or on a word, you are going to focus on your desires. Before you begin to do your meditations, you are going to take a few minutes to focus on your life board. Look at all the images that you want in your life. Get a clear picture so that when you close your eyes you will still retain the images of the choices you've made.

By now you should have a meditation routine established. Begin your normal meditation practice. Light candles or incense and play your background music, if you have it. Only play an instrumental music CD. If you have been using a guided meditation CD up until this point, you don't want to use it now; the words of the CD might interfere with your focus on your own desires. The type of meditation you will be doing now is very specific. Get into a comfortable meditation position. Review the board for a few minutes and then close your eyes.

Inhale deeply. As you exhale, get a clear picture of what you would like to manifest in your life. At the same time say "aaaaahhhhh." Inhale through your nose and repeat. Your goal is eventually to do this for twenty minutes; you can work up to this goal. As you continue this meditation with your life board over the weeks ahead, you will be amazed as things you focus on begin to materialize in your everyday life.

Activity:

❤ Construct your life board.

❤ Meditate on all you wish to manifest in your life.

CHAPTER SIXTEEN

The Dating Guide

"FEAR LESS, HOPE MORE; EAT LESS, CHEW MORE;
WHINE LESS, BREATHE MORE; TALK LESS, SAY MORE;
LOVE MORE, AND ALL GOOD THINGS WILL BE YOURS."

—SWEDISH PROVERB

Congratulations! You made it. You have spent a lot of time and energy. You have worked hard, you have grown, and you have changed. Now you are ready to put all that hard work and energy into use and start dating again. Of course, you are not going to date the way you did before. You have a new way of dating.

Begin by deciding what you want. All systems in the universe are based on energy. If we look at the basic building blocks of all matter, we will find atoms. Atoms bond to each other to make everything we see. This bonding is based on energy. You have a positive and a negative energy. Another way of looking at it is a male and female energy. The male would be the one atom with the electron and the female would be the atom that receives the electron. This sharing of the electron creates the bond—the basis of the science of chemistry.

Relationship chemistry is also based on energy bonding. Most people are familiar with the concept of opposites attracting. This is illustrated in ancient Chinese philosophy by the concept of yin and yang. Yin and yang describe two opposing but complementary aspects of any one phenomenon. Most systems have a yin and a yang. For example, in the seasons, the winter would be considered the yin and summer would be the yang. Yin is considered the female aspect and is characterized as being soft, slower, substantial, tranquil, conserving, and gentle. The yang is considered male and is characterized by heat, fire, restlessness, hardness, dryness, and speed.

Since each human being is a system, we all have both yin and yang characteristics. In fact, some women (and I'm talking about myself here) run into problems because they send out mixed messages of yin and yang. I wanted to be in a relationship, yet maintain my sense of independence. I wanted a man who was strong and powerful, but not at the cost of my feeling weak. At work I expected to be treated like an equal, but when I was at home I wanted to be treated like a lady, with the man in my life bringing me flowers and opening doors for me. The problem was that my competing desires sometimes created confusion.

I remember one particularly painful experience. I had been dating the man for a short period of time, and I enjoyed being with him. He had driven three hours to attend an art exhibition with me. While getting tickets at the box office, I should have been gracious and accepting when he offered to pay. However, I pushed his money back and said, "No, I'll get it." I was trying to show him I appreciated all the effort he had gone through to be with me. But it backfired. The ticket seller reached for my credit card and stated in a nasally, know-it-all voice, "You know, he really should be paying for this!" I cringed; I could feel my date shrinking behind me. I felt terrible. I tried to explain to the ticket seller that he'd tried, but it was too late. My desire to feel independent resulted in uncomfortable tension. At the exhibit he was very sweet, but afterward he didn't want to see me again.

When you return to the dating process you will want to be very clear in your intentions. You have done a lot of work, including making a list of what you want from life and what you want in a partner. After reviewing your lists you must decide if you want to be predominantly male- or female-energy in your next relationship. Energy should not be confused with roles. Some of the activities associated with energies may fit into stereotypical roles, such as the male-energy person paying for dinner. The energy is based more on characteristics than actions.

People are a combination of both male and female energy, but one is usually more dominant in a person. The female energy is characterized by emotion, softness, intuition, and receptiveness. The male energy is characterized by logic, hardness, reasoning, and giving. In the beginning of any relationship you need to make clear which aspect you want to be. A female can choose to be male-energy. A female who has chosen to express male energy in her life would be characterized by calling the shots and having the money. She would not be predominantly emotional but tend to reason logically. She is usually very successful in her business life and may even run a company. The man she blends best with may be more emotional and yielding. He may be an artist or a musician. He will be more passive and allow for her dominance. Does this mean that all successful women need to date passive men? Absolutely not. Remember, we are each a combination of energies. Therefore, we may be very male at work but be very female at home. It is our choice. But whatever we choose, we must be cognizant of that choice. If we decide to be female at home, but come home one day from our work still feeling more logical and competitive, we could inadvertently create a competitive male power struggle at home with our male-energy man.

A male-energy person does not tend to respond well to direct orders. For example, a man might come home and take off his shoes and socks, leaving them on the floor. The female who is having a male-energy moment might say, "I have asked you a million times to pick up your socks." When the male hears this, he has a natural tendency to rebel. He will do everything else but pick up the socks. On the other hand, male-energy people love to problem solve. Present a male-energy person with a situation they can solve, wherein they can be the hero or the heroine, and stand back and watch them shine.

In the beginning, we choose the energy that sets the tone for the rest of the relationship. As the relationship progresses, you may renegotiate your energies, but you need to make a clear choice in the beginning. For example, doing the checking and finance—logical and rational—would be a male-energy activity. However, you may find that while in all other facets your male is a dominant male, banking and balancing the checking account is not his forte. So as the relationship progresses, the female may take over the checking.

Once we decide which energy we would like to be, we must act accordingly.

DATING FEMALE

Dating female is all about receiving. The male chooses the time and place, picks up the female, and pays the check. In fact, if you are dating female, all these items are assumed. You do not even offer to contribute. Dating female means you are looking for a dominant man. A true dominant man will be relieved and happy that there is a woman who "knows how to act like a female" (in his view). He will gladly become attentive, opening doors and pulling out your chair for you. However, if your date has been dating male- or mixed-energy females, he may have become confused. He needs to understand who you are. So if he asks you to choose a restaurant, say something like "Thank you for your confidence, but I would feel more comfortable if you chose." As the female energy, you function off emotion. You do not need to explain yourself. Logical explanation is a male-energy trait. All the female needs to say is "*This is how I feel.*" A true dominant male will respond to this. So if he suggests you go Dutch or that you pay, let him know that this makes you feel uncomfortable and that you feel (not think) that the man should pay (provided this is truly the way you feel).

Allow the male to be dominant. During dinner, allow him to talk. Instead of talking about yourself, ask him general questions. As the female, you respond with how you *feel.* When you ask him questions, you ask him what he *thinks.* You never ask a dominant male how he feels. He thinks, you feel. This does not mean you check your brains at the door. No, dominant males love a strong, independent, intelligent woman who has self-confidence. However, on the first few dates, allow him to be the center of attention. In the competitive world we sometimes like to be one-up on a story. Never do this with a dominant male. When dating female, we want a male who is our hero; allow him the opportunity to shine.

When we date female, we are strong but not pushy. Males love to test boundaries. So although they want to be with a woman whom they can love and cherish, they may still try to become sexual early on. Do not be offended or disappointed. Be flattered that he finds you attractive; hopefully you find him attractive also. As the female energy, it is your job to set sexual boundaries. Remember what you want. Do you want a casual sexual relationship, or are you looking for a long-term, exclusive one? Let him know how you feel. On the first few dates you just need to tell him you don't feel comfortable about having sex with him yet. Let him know you find him very attractive but you want to wait. As you continue to date, explain that you are looking for a long-term, exclusive relationship, and only after you have that will you feel comfortable enough to give yourself to him sexually. A dominant male will respect and appreciate that request. In fact, he may be relieved that he's finally found a female he can trust. Men tend to become leery of a female who becomes sexual too quickly. They wonder, "If she doesn't resist with me, who else isn't she resisting?" A male wants a woman he can trust when he is not around.

DATING MALE

Females who "date male" tend to be career women. They are usually powerful and financially secure. They are more thinking-oriented and less emotional. Dominant males will tend to compete with this type of woman just as they would another male, which may cause problems. Therefore, these women tend to connect better with female-energy males. These males are not intimidated by the female's power or success. Often they are younger than the woman.

The male-energy female will tend to call the shots. She goes after what she wants and usually makes the first move. She will make all the dinner arrangements and usually pays. She may even suggest his attire or pick up an outfit on the way over. The men she dates will be more passive and sensitive, and respect her power.

DATING DIFFERENTLY

Sometimes when we begin to date someone, we realize, "Wow, I really like him." At this point, we may start to feel self-conscious, sometimes to the point of not being able to hear him. Instead of having an easy, enjoyable conversation, we start worrying about what we are going to say in response to what he is saying. We begin to censor or edit our words based on his responses, trying to put the best light on ourselves. Although this is normal, and there is nothing wrong with wanting to be liked, it's not a great idea to date like we are on a job interview. That means we are not going to "sell" ourselves. Also, we need to stop asking interrogating questions.

Patricia was a very pretty woman with an outgoing personality. She had several men ask her out. But she was frustrated with dating because she didn't seem to get past the first date with the men she liked. If she liked them, they never seemed to call for a second date, and if she didn't like them, they tended to always call. And to make matters worse, she felt that her biological clock was ticking and she would very much have liked to be on course to get married and have children before it was "too late."

After reviewing Patricia's dating patterns, it became apparent to me what was causing her own frustration. Once she decided she liked a guy, she turned up her male energy. It was as if she was no longer dating but had launched into a business transaction. She would ask her dates probing and sometimes very uncomfortable questions. After one date, one of the guys said he felt like she was trying to close a sale. What was happening to Patricia is that once she decided that her date was a good candidate, she started asking questions about his job, where he saw himself in the future, whether he wanted to get married and have kids. Instead of relaxing and having fun, the man walked away feeling like she was too pushy and desperate. At the opposite extreme, once she discovered that she didn't particularly care for the man she was with (a "noncandidate"), she relaxed and became her usual outgoing self. This relaxed attitude was appealing, so these were the men who called her for a second date. Her behavior was repelling what she did want and attracting what she didn't.

All Patricia needed to do was simply relax and stop trying to make a decision about who was a candidate and who was a noncandidate on the first date. She is now dating with patience. She is relaxing and having fun. She is taking her time and being herself. She is no longer concerned about deciding if she likes him with her head instead of her heart.

When we date slowly, we date with our hearts and make better decisions. When we date with our heads we tend to size people up too quickly, a little like judging a book by its cover or a new car by the color. We try to determine if he looks good "on paper"—what does he do, where does he live, where did he go to school, does he have a bank account, etc. When we date with our hearts, we spend time with a person and then determine how we feel being around him over a more extended period of time. Many of us rush into a relationship because the man has a great job or an impressive education, lives at a good address, or makes a lot of money. Only later do we discover that we really don't enjoy spending time with him. At the very least, taking it slow increases the likelihood of spending more time with people you really like. And in the process, you are more likely to find "the one."

You are also going to be less concerned about whether or not he likes you as you really are, at your most comfortable. In other words, you are not going to sell yourself; you are going to *be* yourself. If for some strange reason he's just not into you, be grateful and move on. Realize he is freeing you up for someone more appropriate for you. Be gracious and thank him. Recognize that he is not rejecting you; he just realized you and he are not a good fit. Remind yourself constantly that you are looking for your best fit—the right "chemistry." Just like when we walk into a clothing store we all have many choices, some choices fit better than others. When clothing doesn't fit right or doesn't look good when you put it on, that doesn't mean there is anything wrong with the outfit—nor does it mean that something is wrong with you. It just means that one outfit is better suited to your body type, and another outfit is suited to someone else.

You may remember the fairy tale of Cinderella. When she lost her shoe at the ball, the prince found it, and scoured the land for the lady whose foot it would fit; she would become his princess. By this time, Cinderella was back home with her horrible stepmother and stepsisters, who eagerly rushed forward to try on the shoe when the prince's servants came calling. The ugly sisters wanted that prince for themselves, and in some versions of the story, each sister deformed her own foot to make it fit a shoe that didn't belong to her. Only when it became obvious that the little scullery maid in the corner had the right foot to fit the shoe naturally did the real princess win her prince. She didn't have to change parts of herself to "fit" her prince. Neither do you.

YOU ARE THE PRIZE

Remember as you start dating again—you are the prize. Your job is to choose from the best offers. You know he is interested, because he asked you out. Be comfortable and be yourself. When we're not comfortable we tend to try to compensate for our discomfort by assuming roles, maybe even "cutting off" or stuffing down parts of ourselves. If you believe he asked you out because someone said you were sweet and liked to bake, you may be tempted to act more passively or more "domestic" than you really are. It is very important to be yourself. If a date evolves into a relationship, you want to be you. A relationship built on lies—or simply a "good act"—is destined to fail, because you cannot keep up the charade indefinitely. Your own inner turmoil will sabotage the relationship in order to find relief.

Men are creatures of action—they enjoy winning the prize. Remember that you are that prize, and let the man you want be himself and do what it takes to win you. It may take time, but you can be patient and enjoy the effort he expends in trying to achieve you—the prize—for himself.

TAKE YOUR TIME

I know women who spend more time picking out a pair of shoes than they spend picking a potential life partner. This type of woman spots a man across the room. Their eyes meet and that spark of physical attraction draws them together. The next thing you know, they are in bed together. They never took the time to get to know each other, and now that they have slept together they have developed a false sense of intimacy. They may even feel obligated to try to have a long-term relationship since they have been sexual together. After some time, maybe even years, they break up, wondering what they ever saw in each other to begin with. The irony is that this same woman will tell me she doesn't have the time to date slowly—not realizing that dating slowly might have saved her several years of disastrous, or at least unsatisfactory, relationships.

Take your time. Pick and choose. You don't have to choose right away. There is no time limit. You may meet one man who has a lot you like, but you are just not quite sure. Just keep dating—keep dating him and others.

What I've found is that when I say no to the universe, or when I say, "Thank you, but this is not quite what I want," the universe comes back with something better. You are honing your choices. You are saying, "I like this, but I don't like that." You may say, "I like this about that one, and that about another." The next one may have a blend of those qualities. I dated one guy who had time to play, and I enjoyed that. The problem was that he had so much play time because he didn't work very much, so although he had time, his funds were limited. The next guy had more funds, but his time was limited. I kept dating. I eventually met a man who blended the two, a happy medium between time and money.

Remember, you get what you settle for. There is no time limit. If he pressures you into making a decision, then tell him you don't feel ready. The lesson here is that if you have to make a decision today, the answer will have to be no. If he cares about you and the relationship, he will understand and allow you time. If he doesn't understand and he leaves, then he was not the right man for you. If he is going to bully you at the beginning of the relationship, he will only get worse as the relationship progresses. Be grateful he is gone and consider yourself spared.

MEN LIKE MYSTERY

Don't tell him everything about yourself on the first date. In fact, don't tell him everything about yourself, ever. It's kind of like a magic show; we would like to know how the trick is done, but that would detract from our enjoyment of it. We sometimes like to tell all quickly, in order to achieve a degree of intimacy, but this usually backfires. Tell him the big stuff, such as how many marriages, but don't tell him how many boyfriends. A grown man who realizes you are a grown woman will also realize that he is not the first. He doesn't really need to know he's closer to the 101st.

In the beginning, listen. Ask questions, but don't probe. Ask him about his adventures and encourage him to share funny stories, but avoid too many personal questions. Ask open-ended questions such as "What do you do?" When he answers, say, "Wow, that sounds interesting. What is that like?" The irony is that people always feel *you* are more interesting when you are more interested in them.

WHEN YOU THINK YOU HAVE FOUND HIM

He's cute, he's funny, he looks good on paper, and your body really likes him. What to do now? Wait. I cannot emphasize this enough. When we enjoy someone and our bodies want to get physical, waiting can be very difficult. But remember, we are trying to choose a partner. You will hopefully spend the rest of your life with this person. You don't want to make a hasty decision. In the beginning, everyone is on his or her best behavior. Sometimes it takes many dates for the true person to emerge. Keep dating until you are sure. Check your list. Does he have the qualities you want? Are there any deal breakers? Remember, you are now dating differently; you are not going to settle or jump prematurely into a sexual relationship, hoping for the best and believing everything will eventually turn out fine, even the things you don't like about him.

Candace began dating Phil. He was good-looking and funny, and she loved his laid-back attitude. They dated several times, and she began to think he was the one. She was very sexually attracted to him and wanted to bring the relationship to the next level. She had also been dating another man and was inwardly debating about dating Phil exclusively.

One Friday night Phil called around 9:30. They had not planned on seeing each other because he'd said he had to work late. But now he explained that he had finished work and wanted to see if she would like to get together. Normally she would have said no to a late-night request on such short notice, but since she was interested in moving the relationship up a notch, she agreed. Phil arrived at about ten; his eyes were red and glassy. Candace assumed he was tired from working all day. Then he kissed her. There was a strange taste on his breath; he had been smoking pot. He was becoming comfortable enough with her to show his true self.

Candace needed to make a decision. She realized that smoking pot was a deal breaker for her. So, with some difficulty, since she had felt ready to move forward with him, she decided to stop seeing him. Three weeks later she met someone else; she's in a relationship with him now. She says she is so happy she waited and had the courage to follow her heart. She could have settled and tried to make it work with Phil or, worse, try to change him, but she is glad she didn't. Now she is in an incredible relationship with a wonderful man who she never would have dreamed existed.

THE NEXT LEVEL

Okay, so now you have had several dates with a man, and you like him. You have looked over your list and he fits. You've looked at the deal breakers, and he has none of them. You have met his friends, been in his home, and even met his dog. You are so physically attracted to him you can hardly contain yourself. You wonder if it is time to go to the next level and become intimate.

At this point, you need to make it perfectly clear. You want to tell him you are very attracted to him, but to become intimate you need to feel safe. You need to feel that you are in an exclusive, monogamous relationship. You are not asking for a commitment of marriage, but would like to know if marriage is a goal in his future.

If you are both in agreement, then it's time for the next level. Enjoy!

Activity:

♥ Enjoy your new life!

Resources

Central Recovery Press
http://www.centralrecoverypress.com

The Broken Picker-Fixer (Dawn Maslar website)
http://www.brokenpickerfixer.com

Charities on the Better Business Bureau list
http://www.bbb.org/charity-reviews/national

Codependents Anonymous
http://www.coda.org

Dawn's Advice blog on relationships in recovery
http://www.loveintherooms.com

Dawn's past radio shows online archive
http://www.blogtalkradio.com/search/dawn-maslar

Emotions Anonymous
http://emotionsanonymous.org

The Happiness Project
http://www.happiness-project.com

How to Meditate
http://how-to-meditate.org

Indulge yourself
http://www.spafinder.com

Meditation Society of America
http://www.meditationsociety.com

**National Association of Holistic
Aromatherapy (NAHA)**
http://www.naha.org

Physical activity guidelines
http://www.health.gov/paguidelines

Sleep information
http://www.sleepfoundation.org

Tea Council of the USA
http://teausa.org

**US Department of Health and Human Services;
Healthy Marriage Initiative**
http://www.acf.hhs.gov/healthymarriage

**U. S. Government food pyramid
(food guidelines)**
http://www.mypyramid.gov

Yoga Alliance
http://yogalliance.org